Debates on English Education

영어교육토론

2nd edition | 개정판

Debates on English Education

영어교육토론

2nd edition | 개정판

Park Jai Young Ph.D.

한국문화사

Preface

In Korea, English education has long been a subject of intense public interest, policy debate, and academic inquiry. From early childhood immersion programs to the pressures of college entrance exams, English learning touches nearly every aspect of a student's journey. This book, *Debates on English Education* (2nd ed.), is designed to help future teachers critically examine these issues, not only to prepare for the national teacher employment exam but also to become reflective, informed, and empathetic educators.

This revised edition builds on the foundation of the first, and I am pleased to have had the opportunity to improve and expand the content. With more refined arguments, updated perspectives, and clearer organization, my hope is that this second edition will better serve readers who are preparing to become English teachers in Korea's evolving educational landscape.

Each chapter explores a different theme, from early learning and standardized testing to multicultural classrooms, digital tools, and student rights. These are not merely academic concerns but lived realities in Korean schools. Readers are invited to engage with these topics through structured discussion, guided reflection, and debate. Rather than offering final answers, the goal is to cultivate thoughtful inquiry and professional insight.

In the process of writing this book, I also explored emerging tools, including artificial intelligence, as a way to clarify ideas, organize content, and test the accessibility of certain explanations. Just as teachers are learning to integrate AI into education, I, too, found it valuable as a companion in shaping how this book communicates with its readers.

As a professor of English Education, I have seen firsthand the challenges and aspirations of those preparing to enter the classroom. This book is written for you—university students, aspiring teachers, and educators who care deeply about the future of learning in Korea. May it support your growth, deepen your thinking, and guide your journey as a thoughtful and principled teacher.

Contents

Preface		03
How to Use This Book		06

Chapter 1 Little Learners, Big Expectations — Early English Education in Korea 09

Chapter 2 English in Elementary School — Foundation or Burden? 27

Chapter 3 Free Semester and Gap Year — Time to Explore or Waste of Time? 45

Chapter 4 Redesigning High School — Credit System, Grading, and the CSAT Reform 63

Chapter 5 College Admission System — Shaping Students, Shaping Society 81

Chapter 6 Who Owns the Classroom? — Rights, Authority, and Responsibility in School Life 99

Chapter 7 Welcoming Diversity — Multicultural Education in Korean Classrooms 117

Chapter 8 Learning Without Limits — Education for Students with Special Needs 135

Chapter 9 Beyond the Test — Rethinking Education Through the International Baccalaureate Lens 153

Chapter 10 Talking About What Matters — Rethinking Sex Education in a Changing World 175

Chapter 11 College Life Unfiltered — From Club Fairs to Career Fears 193

Chapter 12 AI and the Future of Learning — Promise, Peril, and Possibility 211

Epilogue 229

How to Use This Book

Each chapter in this book follows a consistent structure to guide students through reflection, discussion, and critical thinking:

- **Warm-Up:** Simple, personal questions to activate prior knowledge and introduce the topic. Use these for self-reflection or group conversation.
- **Introduction:** A brief overview of the chapter's theme, combining context, critique, and professional insight. This essay models clear, structured academic writing and offers multiple perspectives.
- **Chitchat with Mates:** Casual discussion prompts meant for group activity. Students can write their own responses and compare with peers to develop conversational English and collaborative thinking.
- **In-Depth Reading:** A longer, analytical essay that provides social context, current issues, and future implications. It serves as the basis for understanding the topic at a deeper level.
- **Comprehension Questions:** Five factual and interpretive questions about the reading. Use these to check understanding, summarize key points, and prepare for written assessments.
- **Ask AI:** A prompt encouraging students to inquire about similar issues in other countries or contexts using AI tools. This section promotes comparative thinking and autonomous research skills. The country mentioned in the prompt is underlined as a suggestion and may be changed to another country of interest.
- **In-Depth Discussion Questions:** Eight open-ended questions that challenge students to analyze, apply, and evaluate the topic. Ideal for class discussions, group debates, or writing practice.
- **Debate:** Four debate topics with "Agree/Disagree" options. These are designed to build argumentation skills and encourage students to consider both sides of complex issues.

- **Wrap-Up:** Your Turn to Write: A final writing prompt that asks students to express their own opinions based on the chapter. A sample student essay is included to model effective organization and reasoning.

- **My Reflections & Notes:** These are open spaces for you to write down key insights, teaching ideas, personal reflections, or any information you want to remember. Use them freely to connect what you've learned to your future role as an educator.

This book can be used in classrooms or for independent study. It aims to help future educators not only improve their English proficiency but also develop the professional language, perspective, and ethics necessary for shaping Korea's educational future.

Chapter 01

Little Learners, Big Expectations — Early English Education in Korea

Warm-Up

- At what age did you first start learning English?
- Do you think it is effective to teach English to children before age 7?
- What are the benefits and drawbacks of learning English early?
- What do your parents or family think about early English education?

Introduction

In Korea, the phrase "the earlier, the better" often defines how parents approach their children's English education. Toddlers are frequently enrolled in English immersion kindergartens or watch English YouTube channels before they can fluently speak Korean. Early English education has become a widespread trend, driven by competitive college admissions, parental anxiety, and a belief that early exposure guarantees future success. Yet, this trend is not without controversy.

The rise of private English kindergartens and costly "English playgroup" classes reflects a booming industry centered around young learners. Eager to give their children a head start, many parents invest heavily in songs, cartoons, native-speaking teachers, and overseas camps. These efforts often rely on the popular but debated theory of the "critical period" in language acquisition that there's an ideal window in early childhood for effective language learning.

However, this enthusiasm faces strong criticism from child development specialists, educational researchers, and teachers. They argue that intense early English instruction may hinder Korean language development, cause cognitive stress, and reduce long-term motivation. Others worry about educational inequality, since only wealthier families can afford these programs. Moreover, early exposure doesn't guarantee lasting fluency without sustained instruction and motivation.

This issue intersects with broader concerns in Korea, such as private education fever, the commercialization of childhood learning, and competing views on raising "global citizens." While some countries delay formal language education until later, Korea's aggressive approach reflects its deep cultural drive for achievement.

Teachers must understand both the educational theories and social pressures behind early English education. Should we promote early exposure or advocate for a more developmentally appropriate start? What is the teacher's role in guiding parents, designing curriculum, and supporting children's emotional well-being? This chapter explores these questions, outlines key debates, and invites you to reflect on your position as an educator.

Chitchat with Mates

1 What do you think motivates parents to start English education at an early age?

	Answers
Me	
Mate 1	
Mate 2	
Mate 3	

2 How would you describe a good English learning environment for a 5-year-old?

	Answers
Me	
Mate 1	
Mate 2	
Mate 3	

3 In your opinion, what kind of English activities would be fun and effective for young children?

	Answers
Me	
Mate 1	
Mate 2	
Mate 3	

4 If you were designing an English class for preschoolers, would you focus more on speaking or listening? Why?

	Answers
Me	
Mate 1	
Mate 2	
Mate 3	

 **In-depth Reading**

The Rising Pressure of Early English Education in Korea

In recent decades, English education has become a central concern in Korean society, not only at the secondary and tertiary levels but increasingly from the earliest years of a child's life. In cafes, playgrounds, and online parenting communities, one can often overhear anxious discussions about when to start English lessons, what kind of playgroups are most effective, and whether native-speaking teachers are worth the cost. This educational anxiety, fueled by global competitiveness and social pressure, has led to the rapid growth of English kindergartens, play-based English classes, and a multi-billion-won private education industry targeting children as young as three. While early exposure to language can bring certain benefits, the pressure-filled environment surrounding early childhood English education in Korea raises important concerns that demand critical reflection from future educators.

English Kindergartens: From Late Start to Early Rush

In the past, English education in Korea typically began in middle school, with formal instruction focusing on grammar and reading. However, with globalization and the rise of neoliberal values in education during the late 1990s and early 2000s, English quickly became associated with opportunity and advancement. The government responded by introducing English in elementary schools as part of the national curriculum in 1997. Over time, however, this public initiative was outpaced by the rapid rise of private institutions offering early English education, well before the public school system engaged with it.

Today, English kindergartens are widespread across Korea's metropolitan areas. These institutions promise immersive English environments, foreign teachers, and fun learning activities. Alongside them, smaller English playgroups, often held in private academies or community centers, offer less formal but equally ambitious alternatives. These programs are marketed to parents as the key to building "native-like" fluency, with heavy emphasis on early exposure to maximize long-term language development. This belief has contributed to a booming market that often functions with limited oversight or standardization.

Parental Anxiety and the Myth of the "Golden Period"

A key driver behind this phenomenon is parental anxiety, rooted in what is often referred to as the myth of the "golden period." This theory suggests that there is a critical window, usually before age seven, when children can acquire languages effortlessly and achieve near-native proficiency. While some linguistic studies support the idea that younger children may pick up pronunciation more easily, many experts argue that meaningful language acquisition requires consistent input, motivation, and cognitive readiness that go beyond age alone.

Parents, however, often internalize the fear of missing this "window," leading to intense competition to start earlier and invest more. In online forums and parenting blogs, stories of five-year-olds reading English books or speaking fluently are widely circulated, feeding unrealistic expectations and a sense of urgency. This anxiety often overlooks the importance of balanced development in a child's emotional, social, and first-language growth.

Child development specialists and education researchers have raised serious concerns about the impact of premature English instruction. First, some children experience linguistic confusion, as their first language (Korean) competes with a foreign language for dominance. This can delay expressive vocabulary, hinder literacy in the first language, and affect identity formation. Moreover, programs that push children into structured academic routines too early may lead to emotional fatigue and reduce intrinsic motivation for learning.

From a pedagogical perspective, the quality of instruction in many private English kindergartens is inconsistent. Some teachers lack training in early childhood education, and the emphasis on English exposure often comes at the expense of play, creativity, and social interaction, all of which are vital for young learners. Without a holistic educational approach, English becomes a performance-oriented goal rather than a meaningful communicative tool.

Global Comparisons: Finland and Japan

A useful lens for analyzing Korea's situation is through international comparison. Finland, for instance, delays formal instruction in both first and foreign languages until the age of seven. Despite this, Finnish students consistently perform well in English proficiency assessments. The focus in early childhood is on play, emotional development, and curiosity, foundations that later support language learning and critical thinking. Teachers are highly trained and trusted, and schools emphasize holistic development over early academic pressure.

Japan, Korea's close neighbor, has also experienced a growing interest in early

English education but tends to integrate it more conservatively into its public education system. While private English kindergartens exist, the level of social pressure and privatization is less intense than in Korea, partly due to stronger regulation and different cultural attitudes toward early education. The Japanese system often prioritizes balanced development and long-term consistency over immediate academic achievement, reducing the sense of urgency seen in Korea's private sector.

Market vs. Public Education: A Growing Divide

One of the most troubling aspects of Korea's early English education trend is the widening gap between private and public education. While wealthier families can afford high-quality English programs, lower-income families are left behind, creating inequities that begin before a child even enters elementary school. Public kindergartens and nurseries, restricted by policy and funding, often avoid English instruction altogether, fearing controversy or inconsistency with national guidelines.

This market-driven system places teachers and public schools in a difficult position. On one hand, they must accommodate students with vastly different levels of English exposure. On the other, they face pressure from parents who expect advanced instruction from the earliest grades, regardless of developmental appropriateness.

A Call for Balance and Developmentally Appropriate Practices

Rather than dismissing early English education altogether, it is more productive to seek a balanced, age-appropriate approach. For very young children, English exposure should be playful, interactive, and non-threatening. Songs, games, storytelling, and body movement are far more effective and emotionally supportive than drills or rote memorization. Above all, early English education should respect a child's developmental stage, promote joy in learning, and support both Korean and English language growth.

Teachers will play a crucial role in reshaping parental expectations, guiding policy implementation, and creating inclusive classrooms where language learning is not a race, but a meaningful journey. The rising pressure for early childhood English education in Korea reflects deep societal values about success, globalization, and competition. While early exposure can have certain benefits, it must be balanced with respect for child development, equity, and educational quality. As future educators, we must move beyond the myth of the "golden period" and advocate for thoughtful, research-informed practices that prioritize children's holistic growth over mere performance. By doing so, we can help shape a healthier and more equitable vision for English education in Korea.

Comprehension Questions

1 What historical changes in Korea led to the early introduction of English education for young children?

2 According to the essay, what are some reasons parents feel pressured to begin English education before elementary school?

3 What concerns do child development experts raise about early English education in Korea?

4 How does the essay compare Korea's early English education approach with that of Finland or Japan?

5 What recommendations does the essay offer for future teachers regarding early childhood English education?

 **Ask AI**

Are English Kindergartens popular in China? Why or why not?

ⓘ In-depth Discussion Questions

1 If a parent of a five-year-old asks you whether they should send their child to an English kindergarten, how would you respond? What key points would you include in your explanation?

2 Imagine you are teaching first grade. Some students have attended English kindergartens, while others have had no English exposure. How would you manage this gap in the classroom without discouraging or overwhelming either group?

3 Have you ever observed or experienced an English class for very young children (ages 3–6)? What did you notice about the teaching style, student reactions, and classroom atmosphere? What seemed effective or problematic?

4 If your future school assigns you to teach a short English playgroup for preschoolers, what kinds of activities would you design? How would you keep the focus on fun and learning at the same time?

_____
_____
_____
_____
_____
_____

5 What kind of pressure do you think parents feel when they hear about other children speaking English fluently at age 5 or 6? How might you, as a teacher, help reduce that pressure or provide realistic advice?

_____
_____
_____
_____
_____
_____

6 In your view, should public kindergartens and daycares include English in their daily routine? Why or why not? What challenges might this cause for teachers and children?

_____
_____
_____
_____
_____
_____

7 Some children who start English very early become bored or resistant to it by the time they reach elementary school. Why do you think this happens, and how can we prevent it as teachers?

8 Think about your own English learning journey. Would you have wanted to start earlier? Why or why not? How might your experience shape the way you teach English to young learners in the future?

9 Make a discussion question based on the information you have obtained for "Ask AI."

◉ Debate

1 Children should not begin formal English education before the age of seven. (Focus: developmental appropriateness vs. early exposure advantage)

Agree	Disagree

2 Private English kindergartens worsen educational inequality and should be more strictly regulated by the government. (Focus: access, equity, and public policy)

Agree	Disagree

3 Early childhood English education is more about parental anxiety than children's actual learning needs. (Focus: societal pressure vs. pedagogical value)

Agree	Disagree

4 Public kindergartens in Korea should offer English classes to reduce the private education gap. (Focus: curriculum design, equity, and practicality in public education)

Agree	Disagree

🖉 Wrap-Up: Your Turn to Write

Prompt: *Do you believe that early English education is beneficial for children in Korea? Why or why not? Share your personal experience and your vision as a teacher.*

_____
_____
_____
_____
_____
_____
_____
_____
_____
_____
_____
_____
_____
_____
_____
_____
_____
_____
_____
_____
_____
_____

Sample Essay

Yes, I believe early English education can be beneficial for children in Korea, but only under the right conditions. Simply exposing children to English at a young age does not automatically lead to fluency or long-term success. What truly matters is how English is taught, how children respond to it, and whether it supports or disrupts their overall development.

From my own experience, I began learning English in elementary school. I often felt I was behind classmates who had been attending private English kindergartens since the age of four. However, I also saw that many of those students grew tired of English or lost motivation as they got older. Their early start did not guarantee better skills in the long run. In fact, some became resistant to English because of pressure from parents or repetitive instruction.

As a future teacher, I believe early English education should be playful, age-appropriate, and enjoyable. Young learners should not be pressured to memorize vocabulary or study grammar. Instead, they should learn through singing, storytelling, and interactive games. The goal is not academic performance but building positive feelings toward the language.

I also believe teachers have a responsibility to guide parents. Many parents invest heavily in private English education due to social pressure or fear of falling behind. As educators, we must help parents understand that healthy language learning takes time and that emotional well-being is more important than early academic achievement. Early English education can be valuable, but only when guided by respect for the child.

◉ My Reflections and Notes

Write down key insights, teaching ideas, personal reflections, or any information you want to remember.

Chapter 02

English in Elementary School — Foundation or Burden?

Warm-Up

- What grade did you start learning English in public school, and what do you remember about that experience?

- Do you think English is one of the most important subjects in elementary school? Why or why not?

- How do Korean elementary schools usually teach English? What methods have you seen or experienced?

- What are some challenges elementary students face when learning English for the first time?

Introduction

In South Korea, English is formally introduced in the third grade of elementary school as part of the national curriculum. The government's intention behind this early instruction is to foster students' basic communication skills, mainly listening and speaking, through engaging, interactive methods. English is not tested through high-stakes exams at this stage, allowing students to build confidence and enjoy the learning experience without the fear of failure. The hope is that early exposure can reduce resistance to English in later years and serve as a stepping stone to future fluency.

However, the role and effectiveness of English education in elementary schools have become increasingly debated. As English continues to play a powerful role in Korea's academic hierarchy, college admissions, and job market, questions are being raised about whether elementary-level instruction serves as a healthy foundation or an early burden.

Supporters argue that early English education helps children develop better pronunciation, listening skills, and familiarity with basic sentence structures. Children are more open to learning new sounds and less self-conscious about making mistakes at a younger age. A fun and encouraging English class in elementary school may spark lifelong interest in language learning and global communication. Some even view this early education as essential for preparing students for the rapidly globalizing world.

Critics, however, raise valid concerns. The disparity between students who receive private English education, often starting in preschool, and those who rely solely on public school classes is growing. This inequality creates a classroom gap where some students are far ahead, while others struggle to keep up. The psychological effects can be significant: frustration, embarrassment, and a loss of confidence in English. Teachers are often left to deal with wide ability differences in large classrooms, without adequate support or training in differentiated instruction.

Moreover, there is growing debate over whether English should be a priority at this stage, given the importance of Korean literacy, emotional development, and foundational thinking skills. Should English instruction be delayed, or should we rethink how it's taught?

😀 Chitchat with Mates

1 What was your favorite English activity when you were in elementary school? Why did you enjoy it?

	Answers
Me	
Mate 1	
Mate 2	
Mate 3	

2 Do you think English classes in public elementary schools are fun and helpful for students today? Why or why not?

	Answers
Me	
Mate 1	
Mate 2	
Mate 3	

3 If you were an elementary school English teacher, how would you help students who feel left behind?

	Answers
Me	
Mate 1	
Mate 2	
Mate 3	

4 How can teachers make English enjoyable for young learners without making it feel like a burden?

	Answers
Me	
Mate 1	
Mate 2	
Mate 3	

📖 In-depth Reading

Early Exposure: A Strong Foundation?

In today's globalized world, the importance of English as an international language is widely acknowledged. In the Republic of Korea, English is more than a subject; it is a symbol of academic excellence, economic mobility, and global readiness. As a result, the government introduced English as a formal subject in the national curriculum starting from third grade in elementary school. The goal is to expose students early to basic English listening and speaking skills through enjoyable and interactive classroom activities. However, this policy has sparked continuous debate among educators, parents, and researchers: is English education at the elementary level truly beneficial, or does it place an unnecessary burden on young learners?

Advocates for early English education often point to the "younger is better" argument. Linguistic research suggests that young children may acquire pronunciation and intonation more naturally due to their developing phonological sensitivity. In classrooms where English is taught through songs, games, storytelling, and gestures, students are more likely to associate the language with fun and curiosity rather than fear or stress. A well-designed elementary English class can foster confidence, reduce anxiety, and build a positive attitude toward learning a foreign language.

Supporters also emphasize the long-term academic benefits. Early exposure allows for a longer period of language acquisition, potentially leading to higher proficiency over time. In an increasingly competitive society like Korea, students who gain comfort with English from an early age may have an advantage not only in school but also in job markets, study abroad opportunities, and international communication. Policymakers, therefore, argue that early English education is a necessary response to the demands of globalization.

Challenges in the Classroom

Despite these advantages, the realities inside the classroom are far more complex. One major challenge is the diversity in student proficiency levels. Some students enter third grade already having attended private English academies (*hagwons*) or English kindergartens since preschool. Others may be encountering English for the first time. This gap results in mixed-ability classrooms, making it extremely difficult for teachers to balance their lessons. Students with higher proficiency may feel bored and unchallenged, while beginners may feel frustrated or embarrassed, which can damage their motivation and self-esteem.

Another issue is that teachers are not always sufficiently trained to teach English, especially in the lower grades. While specialized English teachers are assigned in some schools, many elementary generalist teachers are expected to deliver English lessons with limited support or fluency themselves. This often leads to inconsistent teaching quality, with some classes relying heavily on scripted dialogues or textbook drills rather than meaningful communication.

Psychological Pressure and an Education Gap

English, despite being introduced in elementary school without grading pressure, is not free from emotional weight. Students quickly become aware of the social value of English proficiency, especially when they hear their peers speak fluently or when parents emphasize the importance of private tutoring. This creates a hidden competition, even at an early age.

Children who feel they are "bad at English" may internalize a sense of failure that stays with them throughout their school years. This is especially dangerous at a developmental stage when students are forming their academic self-concept. When English becomes a source of shame rather than curiosity, it becomes a burden. Emotional well-being must be considered when deciding how and when to introduce foreign languages in the curriculum.

One of the most debated aspects of English education in Korea is the inequality between public and private sectors. While the public school system offers English education from grade 3 with limited hours per week, many students attend private academies where they receive more intensive instruction, often by native speakers. This results in a significant disparity not only in language skills but also in confidence and class participation.

Students from wealthier families who can afford private education tend to perform better, while others fall behind. This creates a cycle of educational inequality that begins not in high school or even middle school, but as early as elementary education. Teachers are placed in a difficult position as they must serve both advanced and struggling learners within the same limited instructional time, often with no support for individualized learning plans.

Rethinking the Curriculum

So, is English in elementary school a necessary foundation or an early burden? The answer may depend less on whether it is taught, and more on how it is taught. If early English education focuses on play, communication, and cultural curiosity, it can lay a positive foundation for lifelong learning. However, if it becomes test-oriented, comparative, or a means of competition, it risks becoming emotionally and academically harmful.

Several reforms have been suggested by educators and researchers. These include:

- Delaying formal English instruction to upper elementary grades, while allowing optional exposure through music, story time, or after-school clubs for younger students.
- Improving teacher training so that all elementary teachers are equipped to teach basic communicative English.
- Reducing reliance on textbooks and incorporating more project-based, experiential learning methods.
- Limiting private tutoring pressure through public education reforms that make school English more meaningful and engaging.
- Providing extra support for students with little prior exposure to English, including after-school programs or team teaching models.

Vision for Future Teachers

As teachers, it is crucial to approach English education with empathy, awareness, and creativity. Teachers must be prepared to handle mixed-level classrooms, design inclusive activities, and reassure students who feel left behind. They also have the power to reshape how students perceive English from a burden they must bear to a tool they enjoy using. Building a safe, supportive classroom atmosphere where students are not afraid to make mistakes is essential for nurturing a positive relationship with the language.

Rather than pushing for early fluency or competition, teachers can focus on helping students feel comfortable, curious, and capable. That shift in attitude may prove more important in the long run than any vocabulary test or pronunciation drill. When children see English as a means of expression and connection, not just a subject to master, they are more likely to stay motivated and engaged.

Teachers can also serve as mediators between school and home, helping parents develop realistic expectations and guiding them toward healthy, developmentally appropriate learning choices. In a society as education-driven as Korea, educators have an essential role in turning early English education from a pressure-filled race into an engaging, inclusive, and equitable experience that supports both academic growth and emotional well-being.

Comprehension Questions

1 What are some potential benefits of starting English education in elementary school, according to the essay?

2 What emotional or psychological effects can early English education have on students who feel left behind?

3 Why is the gap between public and private English education a major concern in Korean elementary schools?

4 How does the quality and training of English teachers affect the success of early English education programs?

5 According to the essay, what changes could improve the current English education system in elementary schools?

 **Ask AI**

How do elementary schools teach English in Germany?

❓ In-depth Discussion Questions

1 How can elementary English teachers effectively support both advanced learners who received private education and beginners who are encountering English?

2 What challenges do generalist elementary teachers face when they are asked to teach English without specialized training? What kind of professional development would be most helpful?

3 In your opinion, what is the ideal balance between Korean language development and English exposure in grades 3–6? How can this balance be maintained in practice?

4 How might early negative experiences with English in elementary school affect a student's long-term attitude toward language learning? How can teachers prevent this?

5 What specific classroom activities or lesson designs could make English classes more engaging and less stressful for elementary students? Provide examples.

6 To what extent should English learning in elementary school be linked to real-world communication rather than textbook content? What role can teachers play in this shift?

7 How does parental pressure influence elementary students' attitudes toward English? What can teachers do to help parents adopt a more supportive and realistic mindset?

8 If you were tasked with revising the national English curriculum for grades 3–6, what changes would you propose to make it more equitable, inclusive, and developmentally appropriate?

9 Make a discussion question based on the information you have obtained for "Ask AI."

🗨 Debate

1 English should not be a required subject in elementary school until grade 5. (Focus: developmental readiness vs. early exposure)

Agree	Disagree

2 Public school English classes cannot compete with private academies and should be supplemented by after-school programs. (Focus: educational equity, practicality, and system reform)

Agree	Disagree

3 The current English curriculum for elementary students focuses too much on memorization and not enough on communication. (Focus: curriculum goals and classroom practice)

Agree	Disagree

4 General classroom teachers should not be required to teach English unless they are fully trained language specialists. (Focus: teacher competence, student outcomes, and training policy)

Agree	Disagree

⚡ Wrap-Up: Your Turn to Write

Prompt: *Do you think English education in elementary school is more helpful or harmful? Reflect on your experiences, insights from this chapter, and your future goals as a teacher.*

Sample Essay

I believe English education in elementary school can be helpful, but only when it is developmentally appropriate and inclusive. Starting English in third grade gives students a chance to become familiar with the language early on, but the way it is taught matters more than the age at which it begins.

As a student, I remember feeling both excited and anxious about English. Some of my classmates had already attended private academies or studied abroad, and I struggled to keep up. This created a sense of shame and made me think I wasn't good at languages. Looking back, I realize the problem wasn't English itself, but the comparison and pressure inside the classroom.

As a future teacher, I want to create an English classroom where students feel safe, curious, and supported. I will use interactive methods like songs, games, and role-plays to help students enjoy English without fear of making mistakes. I also want to be aware of the differences in students' English backgrounds and design lessons that include everyone.

Rather than focusing on grammar or fast results, I believe elementary English education should help students build confidence and develop a positive attitude toward language learning. If students enjoy learning English at a young age, they are more likely to stay motivated and succeed later. In the end, English in elementary school can be a strong foundation, but only if we teach with care, flexibility, and empathy.

💡 My Reflections and Notes

Write down key insights, teaching ideas, personal reflections, or any information you want to remember.

Chapter 03

Free Semester and Gap Year — Time to Explore or Waste of Time?

Warm-Up

- What do you know about the "free semester" system in Korean middle schools?
- Have you ever participated in a program that focused on projects or career exploration in school?
- Do you think students should have time to explore their interests during school years? Why or why not?
- What is the main purpose of education—getting good grades or discovering your future path?

Introduction

In 2016, South Korea implemented the Free Semester System in all middle schools. Typically held in the first year, this semester suspends written exams and traditional test-based evaluations. Instead, students engage in project-based learning, career exploration, club activities, and presentations. The goal is to reduce academic stress and help students explore their interests and aptitudes in a more holistic, student-centered way.

Though the policy's intention is widely supported, opinions on its effectiveness remain divided. Supporters believe it helps students discover strengths, build communication, and develop critical thinking—skills often overlooked in exam-focused classrooms. It also promotes creativity, teamwork, and real-world application. Educators in many OECD countries have praised it as a progressive step toward lifelong learning competencies.

However, critics argue the program lacks depth, structure, and tangible outcomes. Some schools struggle to create meaningful experiences due to limited resources, overworked staff, or weak community involvement. As a result, students may see the semester as unproductive or even pointless. Since exams resume the next semester, many parents and students remain skeptical, fearing it could weaken discipline or harm long-term academic competitiveness.

Student motivation is another concern. Without exams, some disengage if the school fails to offer structured, engaging alternatives. This risks turning an innovative model into a symbolic gesture. Success relies on school leadership, teacher creativity, and community support, all of which vary across the country.

Globally, a similar idea appears in the "gap year." In the UK, Australia, and increasingly the U.S., students often take a year off after high school for travel, internships, or work. Advocates say it builds maturity, independence, and informed decision-making. Like Korea's Free Semester, the gap year shifts focus from academic pressure to personal growth.

This chapter examines both systems as alternative learning periods. Do they offer genuine opportunities, or are they idealistic experiments that fall short? How can Korean educators ensure these programs become meaningful, not missed chances?

😊 Chitchat with Mates

1 If you had experienced a free semester in middle school, what kind of project or activity would you have liked to try?

	Answers
Me	
Mate 1	
Mate 2	
Mate 3	

2 Do you think a gap year after high school could be helpful for Korean students? Why or why not?

	Answers
Me	
Mate 1	
Mate 2	
Mate 3	

3 What are some non-academic skills students should learn during school?

	Answers
Me	
Mate 1	
Mate 2	
Mate 3	

4 If exams disappeared for one semester, how would most students in Korea react? Would they use the time meaningfully?

	Answers
Me	
Mate 1	
Mate 2	
Mate 3	

📖 In-depth Reading

A Shift Toward Holistic Learning

In an education system long dominated by high-stakes exams and rote memorization, South Korea's *free semester system* represents a bold shift in values. Introduced nationwide in 2016, the policy allows middle school students, typically in their first year, to spend one semester free from written tests and performance-based grading. Instead, students participate in project-based learning, club activities, presentations, and career exploration programs. The goal is to encourage creativity, critical thinking, and self-directed learning while relieving the academic pressure that often begins too early in Korean students' lives.

At first glance, this initiative seems progressive and student-centered. Indeed, the free semester has been praised by many educators for its attempt to broaden the definition of meaningful education. Rather than focusing on short-term test scores, it aims to help students discover their interests, improve communication skills, and foster motivation that lasts beyond middle school. Students may take part in theater performances, science experiments, coding workshops, or even job-shadowing experiences. These activities are designed to enhance real-world skills and promote lifelong learning attitudes—goals often overlooked in exam-oriented classrooms.

Problems in Implementation

However, critics argue that the system's implementation is uneven and sometimes superficial. Many schools, especially those in rural or under-resourced areas, struggle to design meaningful experiences due to a lack of funding, community partnerships, or teacher training. In some cases, the semester becomes little more than a break from academic routines without offering real alternatives. When schools fail to provide engaging or purposeful programs, students may view the semester as a vacation or even lose motivation altogether.

Another issue is parental skepticism. In Korea's highly competitive education culture, many parents fear that one semester without exams could leave their children behind in the race for elite high schools and universities. Without grades to measure progress, some parents feel uncertain about their child's learning. As a result, some students continue attending private academies after school during the free semester to maintain their academic edge, which undermines the purpose of the program.

This tension reflects a deeper cultural divide: should education focus on long-term personal growth or short-term academic success? While the Ministry of Education promotes holistic learning, many parents and students remain trapped in a system where test scores define future opportunities. Until college entrance criteria shift to value diverse competencies over test results, programs like the free semester may struggle to gain full public trust.

Global Comparisons: The Gap Year

The concept of taking time off from structured academics is not unique to Korea. In many Western countries, especially the UK and Australia, students are encouraged to take a *gap year* after high school. During this year, students often travel, volunteer, work, or explore personal interests before entering university. Supporters of the gap year argue that it gives students time to mature, reflect on their goals, and develop life skills that classroom learning alone cannot provide. Research shows that students who take a gap year often return to school more motivated and perform better academically than their peers who enroll immediately.

In contrast, gap years are not widely accepted in Korea. The fear of "falling behind" and the stigma of taking a non-traditional path still dominate public opinion. Many students who take a year off after high school do so involuntarily, often to retake the university entrance exam, rather than to explore personal growth. The idea of voluntarily stepping away from academics to rest or discover one's interests is still foreign to many Korean families.

Yet, both the free semester and the gap year share a common purpose: to create breathing room in a system that often suffocates individuality and emotional well-being. They offer time for students to ask important questions: *Who am I? What am I interested in? What kind of future do I want?* These are questions that exams can't answer, but which may define one's direction in life.

The Teacher's Role in Meaningful Reform

As educators, it is important to consider how we can support these programs more effectively. Rather than seeing the free semester as a distraction from academic goals, we must see it as a complementary space for students to build the soft skills, self-awareness, and intrinsic motivation that test-based instruction often fails to cultivate. This requires effort from all sides, teachers who are willing to be facilitators of exploration, schools that are open to flexible curricula, communities that welcome student involvement, and policymakers who support innovation with real resources. Teachers, in particular, must be empowered through training, collaboration, and autonomy to design experiences that connect with students' lives. They play a key role not just in delivering lessons, but in cultivating a learning culture where curiosity, experimentation, and growth are actively encouraged.

Redefining Success in Education

We must also reframe how success is defined in Korean education. Not every valuable outcome can be measured by a score. When students collaborate on a science project, give a presentation, or reflect on a job-shadowing experience, they are engaging in real, meaningful learning, even if it doesn't appear on a transcript. Likewise, students who take time off before university to work or volunteer should not be seen as falling behind, but as gaining perspective that will enrich their academic and personal lives. Success should be seen not only in measurable achievements, but also in the development of adaptable, self-directed individuals who are confident in their identities and prepared for a complex, changing world.

Making Room for Becoming

Ultimately, education is not just about what we know but about who we become. The free semester and the gap year both offer time for students to explore, experiment, and grow beyond the limits of textbooks and exams. These periods allow students to reflect on their identity, interests, and goals, which are often neglected in test-focused environments. They encourage curiosity, resilience, and independence, which are qualities essential for navigating an unpredictable future. As teachers, we must protect and nurture these spaces so that students can breathe, dream, and build lives that are not only successful but also fulfilling. This means listening to students' voices, designing experiences that connect learning with life, and promoting a culture where growth is measured not just by scores but by self-awareness and purpose. If used meaningfully, the free semester and gap year can plant seeds of lifelong learning and personal development, lessons that will last far beyond school.

🔍 Comprehension Questions

1 What are the main goals of Korea's free semester system, and how is it different from traditional education?

2 What are some challenges schools face in implementing the free semester system effectively?

3 Why do some parents remain skeptical about the value of the free semester?

4 How is the idea of a gap year in countries like the UK or Australia different from how time off is viewed in Korea?

5 According to the essay, how should teachers and schools redefine educational success in the context of the free semester or gap year?

 **Ask AI**

Is the gap year popular in Denmark? Why or why not?

In-depth Discussion Questions

1 Have you observed or participated in a free semester program? What worked well, what didn't, and how would you improve it in your future classroom?

2 How can teachers design project-based or experiential learning activities that are meaningful, age-appropriate, and connected to real-world skills and interests?

3 What kinds of training, collaboration, or resources do teachers need to successfully guide students during the free semester and ensure lasting impact?

4 What are the educational risks if the free semester becomes poorly structured or treated merely as a "break" from academic pressure by schools or students?

5 In what ways might a gap year after high school help Korean students discover their passions, build confidence, and reduce long-term academic burnout?

6 How can schools and teachers help parents understand the long-term benefits of the free semester or gap year, especially when there are no immediate test results?

7 As a teacher, how would you balance strict parental expectations for academic achievement with your belief in holistic and student-centered learning experiences?

8 If you could fully redesign the free semester curriculum, what subjects, projects, or community experiences would you include, and why would they matter?

9 Make a discussion question based on the information you have obtained for "Ask AI."

Debate

1 The free semester system in Korean middle schools is more symbolic than effective. (Focus: whether its impact is real or superficial)

Agree	Disagree

2 Taking a gap year after high school helps students mature and should be encouraged in Korea. (Focus: personal growth vs. falling behind academically)

Agree	Disagree

3 Removing exams for one semester harms academic discipline and long-term student performance. (Focus: whether structure or exploration is more important at that age)

Agree	Disagree

4 Free semesters should be optional, not mandatory, so schools can focus on academic excellence if they choose. (Focus: school autonomy vs. systemic change for all)

Agree	Disagree

⚡ Wrap-Up: Your Turn to Write

Prompt: *Do you believe the free semester help students grow, or are they a waste of valuable academic time? Consider your experiences, this chapter's content, and your future role as a teacher.*

Sample Essay

I believe the free semester in Korean middle schools has great potential if used correctly. Instead of constant test preparation, students are given time to explore their interests, try new activities, and learn in creative ways. During this time, students may discover talents or passions that do not appear in traditional classroom settings. I didn't experience a free semester myself, but I remember how stressful school felt. I would have appreciated even one semester focused on learning without pressure.

The main value of the free semester is that it offers students time to ask important questions: What do I enjoy? What am I good at? What kind of future do I want? These questions are not part of a regular exam, but they are essential for building purpose and motivation. When students are encouraged to think beyond tests, they often become more engaged, confident, and self-aware.

However, the effectiveness of the program depends on how schools implement it. If the activities are poorly planned or not engaging, students may just waste time or feel bored. Teachers need support, resources, and training to design meaningful project-based learning experiences. Without this, the free semester becomes a break with no long-term benefit.

As a future teacher, I want to make sure students feel that learning can be exciting and purposeful. I would use the free semester to introduce group projects, real-world problem solving, career exploration, and student reflection journals. I also believe that helping students discover their strengths and passions early can reduce future academic stress and burnout.

Education should be more than test scores. The free semester is not perfect, but it's a step toward creating a school culture where students can breathe, grow, and find direction in their lives. If supported well, it can be a life-changing experience, not just a break from exams.

💡 My Reflections and Notes

Write down key insights, teaching ideas, personal reflections, or any information you want to remember.

Chapter 04

Redesigning High School — Credit System, Grading, and the CSAT Reform

Warm-Up

- What subjects did you enjoy the most in high school, and why?
- Were you ever frustrated by the fixed class schedule in school?
- What do you know about the high school credit system being implemented in Korea?
- Do you think the 5-grade system in high schools is fairer than the previous 9-grade system?

Introduction

In recent years, Korean education has entered a new phase of transformation, especially at the high school level. At the heart of this change is the introduction of the high school credit system, which aims to give students more autonomy in designing their own academic paths. Unlike the traditional one-size-fits-all curriculum, this new system allows students to choose subjects based on their interests, abilities, and future career goals. Inspired by international models such as the American and Finnish systems, the credit system represents a shift toward more personalized and competency-based learning.

At the same time, Korea's grading system has also undergone significant change. The high school transcript now uses a 5-grade system, which ranks students into broad performance categories to reduce excessive competition. Meanwhile, the College Scholastic Ability Test (CSAT) continues to use a 9-grade scale, creating a disconnect between school performance and college admission. This dual system can be confusing for students and may lead to strategic behavior, such as avoiding difficult subjects or focusing only on CSAT-related material.

The challenge becomes even greater when we consider the 2028 CSAT reform, which is expected to further emphasize reasoning and reduce reliance on rote memorization. The reform will also feature a more integrated format for social studies and science, where students will take combined subjects rather than selecting from numerous individual electives. However, without clear changes in university admission policies, students may still feel trapped between two systems—one that encourages exploration and another that demands standardization.

In this chapter, we will explore how these changes are reshaping the high school experience in Korea. We will look at both the promises and problems of the credit system, the implications of mixed grading standards, and the potential impact of the 2028 CSAT. As future educators, you are invited to reflect on what kind of learning environment best supports student growth in a rapidly changing world.

👤 Chitchat with Mates

1 What kind of subjects do you wish had been offered at your high school, and why?

	Answers
Me	
Mate 1	
Mate 2	
Mate 3	

2 How would you feel if your friend got the same grade in the 5-grade system as you, even though you studied harder?

	Answers
Me	
Mate 1	
Mate 2	
Mate 3	

3 Have you ever taken a subject you didn't like just because it was important for university entrance?

	Answers
Me	
Mate 1	
Mate 2	
Mate 3	

4 Do you think a flexible curriculum can really reduce the pressure students feel in high school? Why or why not?

	Answers
Me	
Mate 1	
Mate 2	
Mate 3	

 **In-depth Reading**

A New Direction in Korean Education

Korean education is standing at a turning point. For decades, the system has been marked by rigid curricula, uniform instruction, and relentless pressure to succeed on the College Scholastic Ability Test (CSAT). However, a new educational vision is gradually taking shape—one that emphasizes student choice, diverse learning pathways, and holistic growth. Central to this change is the high school credit system, an ambitious reform that seeks to redefine how Korean students learn and how their achievements are recognized.

The credit system breaks away from the traditional mold of uniform subject delivery. Instead of requiring all students to study the same subjects in the same way, the new model introduces a structure in which students accumulate credits for each completed course, much like in university. This approach encourages students to design their own learning journey, selecting subjects that align with their interests, strengths, or career goals. The shift reflects a growing understanding that no single educational path fits all learners and that a flexible, interest-driven curriculum can lead to deeper engagement and long-term success.

Learning from Canada: A Model of Flexibility

Countries such as Canada have long demonstrated the value of a flexible and student-centered education model. In Canadian high schools, students have considerable autonomy to select from a wide range of academic and vocational courses based on their interests and career goals. A student passionate about the arts may pursue courses in visual design, drama, or creative writing, while another with a STEM—science, technology, engineering, and mathematics—focus can explore physics, engineering, and computer science. This system is supported by well-qualified teachers, comprehensive career counseling, and a school culture that values inclusivity, exploration, and personal development. Korean policymakers, inspired by such approaches, envision a future where Korean students can similarly discover and pursue their strengths in a more adaptive and diversified educational environment.

The 5-Grade Grading System: Reducing Pressure, Raising Concerns

However, introducing this credit system into the Korean context has not been without complications. One of the most significant challenges lies in the way students are evaluated. Alongside the credit reform, the Korean government introduced a new 5-grade system to replace the previous 9-grade ranking within schools. This system divides students into broader categories based on academic performance, such as the top 10% receiving Grade 1, the next 24% Grade 2, then 32% Grade 3, and so on. The purpose was to reduce excessive competition and psychological stress among students, allowing more room for cooperative learning and self-directed exploration.

Yet, in practice, the 5-grade system has brought new concerns. With broader grading bands, it becomes harder for students to distinguish themselves academically, especially in the context of university admissions. Two students at different schools might both receive Grade 2, though their actual performance levels may differ greatly. This makes comparisons across schools more difficult and leads some to suspect grade inflation or inconsistencies. For ambitious students aiming for top universities, the lack of fine differentiation can be frustrating, even demotivating.

The 9-Grade CSAT: A Mismatch with School Assessment

The tension becomes more pronounced when this school-based evaluation is placed beside the CSAT, which still uses the older 9-grade system. The CSAT remains Korea's most influential gateway to higher education, and its structure is fundamentally different from that of the high school grading system. It ranks students based on narrow percentile bands, identifying only the top 4% as Grade 1, the next 7% as Grade 2, then 12% as Grade 3, and so on. This precise ranking can feel at odds with the broader categories used in schools, creating a sense of disconnection between what students learn during the school year and what they are tested on during this high-stakes examination.

Because of this mismatch, students and parents often feel caught between two systems. On one hand, the school curriculum is becoming more flexible and personalized. On the other, university entrance still largely depends on a standardized, competitive test. This gap leads many students to prioritize CSAT preparation over genuine exploration, even if the curriculum allows them to choose electives in music, coding, or global issues. The credit system promises autonomy, but the reality of admissions pressure can strip that autonomy away.

CSAT 2028 Reform: Toward Better Alignment?

The government's reform of the CSAT, scheduled for 2028, aims to bridge this gap. According to the Ministry of Education, the new CSAT will reduce its focus on memorization and emphasize reasoning, interpretation, and literacy. It will incorporate more questions derived from elective and career-related subjects, allowing students' course selections to be reflected in the test. There is also a plan to loosen the tight linkage to state-run materials like EBS, in hopes of promoting more authentic learning.

These changes suggest an effort to align university admissions with the credit system's spirit. However, educators and experts remain cautious. Canada's success with curricular flexibility was not achieved overnight; it is the result of sustained investment in teacher training, curriculum development, and student support. In Korea, unequal access to high-quality instruction and elective subjects is already emerging as a problem. While some urban schools are able to offer a wide range of electives and specialized teachers, smaller or rural schools may struggle to do the same. This imbalance threatens the equity the system claims to support.

Moreover, the new model introduces psychological and developmental challenges. Students, some as young as 15, are now expected to make decisions about their academic focus with long-term consequences. In theory, this allows for early career exploration. In reality, it may pressure students to think strategically rather than authentically. A student who loves history might hesitate to choose it if math offers more secure university pathways. Similarly, students may avoid difficult or highly competitive subjects, fearing that their grades might suffer under the 5-grade system. These decisions can undermine the very goals of the reform.

Equity concerns further complicate the picture. While some urban schools are well-funded and can offer a wide variety of elective subjects with qualified teachers, others, particularly in rural or under-resourced areas, struggle to provide even the basic range of options. This creates a two-tiered system in which students at well-equipped schools enjoy the full benefits of credit-based learning, while their peers elsewhere are limited to a narrow curriculum. Without access to meaningful choices, the promise of student agency becomes a privilege rather than a universal right. This undermines the reform's objective of expanding educational opportunity and increases the risk of deepening educational inequality.

Reform with Responsibility

In summary, Korea's credit-based high school reform is a bold and hopeful attempt to reshape the future of learning. It reflects a broader global shift toward personalized education, creativity, and student agency. Yet, the path forward is complex. Without consistent grading policies, equitable access to electives, university-level reform, and sustained teacher support, the new system risks deepening confusion rather than expanding opportunity. For future educators, understanding these dynamics is not just a policy issue; it's a professional responsibility. In the coming years, they will play a key role in guiding students through a landscape that demands both freedom and clarity, both exploration and structure.

Comprehension Questions

1 What is the main goal of Korea's high school credit system, and how is it similar to Canada's approach?

2 How does the 5-grade system aim to reduce student stress, and what problems has it caused?

3 Why is there a disconnect between the 5-grade system in schools and the 9-grade CSAT?

4 What changes are planned for the 2028 CSAT, and how might they support the credit system?

5 What equity issues are raised by the implementation of the credit system in different types of schools?

 **Ask AI**

How does the credit system work in high schools in New Zealand?

❓ In-depth Discussion Questions

1 How can teachers help students make informed and meaningful subject choices in a credit-based system, especially when they are unsure of their future goals?

2 What strategies can be used to prevent students from avoiding difficult subjects just to protect their grades under the 5-grade system?

3 In what ways might the disconnect between the school grading system (5-grade) and CSAT's 9-grade system impact student motivation and classroom teaching?

4 How should teacher training change to prepare educators for personalized learning, differentiated instruction, and expanded career guidance responsibilities?

5 Is it realistic to expect all schools—regardless of size, location, or funding—to provide a wide range of electives under the credit system? How can we address this disparity?

6 How might the credit system affect students' views of English education, especially when CSAT English still emphasizes reading over communication?

7 Do you think the 2028 CSAT reform will successfully support the goals of the credit system? What further changes might be necessary to align them?

8 What are the risks of implementing a system that gives more freedom to students without first ensuring adequate support, guidance, and infrastructure?

9 Make a discussion question based on the information you have obtained for "Ask AI."

🎤 Debate

1 The CSAT should be abolished and replaced with a portfolio-based admission system that reflects students' performance in credit-based learning. (Focus: standardized testing vs. holistic portfolio evaluation)

Agree	Disagree

2 The 5-grade grading system reduces academic stress but makes university admissions less fair and transparent. (Focus: lower student stress vs. fair academic evaluation)

Agree	Disagree

3 Only schools that can offer a minimum number of elective subjects should be allowed to operate the high school credit system. (Focus: equal access for all schools vs. quality control in implementation)

Agree	Disagree

4 In the Korean context, giving students full autonomy in subject choice at an early age may do more harm than good. (Focus: student freedom and self-direction vs. risk of immature decision-making)

Agree	Disagree

ⓘ Wrap-Up: Your Turn to Write

Prompt: *In your opinion, what is the biggest challenge or opportunity of the high school credit system in Korea, and how should teachers, students, or schools respond to it?*

Sample Essay

In my opinion, the biggest challenge of the high school credit system in Korea is the unequal access to courses and resources. The system gives students more freedom to choose subjects based on their interests and goals. However, this only works well in schools that can offer many different electives. In reality, students in big cities have more options and better facilities, while those in rural or small schools often have limited choices. This makes the system unfair, even though it was created to give students more control over their learning.

To solve this problem, I believe the role of teachers becomes more important than ever. Teachers need to guide students in making realistic and meaningful choices. Even if the school offers fewer subjects, teachers can help students find connections between their interests and the available curriculum. For example, if a school cannot offer a law class, a teacher might integrate legal topics into a social studies project or after-school club. In this way, students can still explore their interests even without a formal elective.

Also, schools must use online resources and digital platforms more actively. Online learning can help small schools offer more subjects without hiring many new teachers. If well managed, this can support equity across regions. The government should also provide financial and technological support to schools that need it.

Overall, the high school credit system has great potential, but only if the playing field is fair. As a future teacher, I want to help my students make the best of their opportunities, regardless of where they go to school. I believe that with strong teacher support and smart use of resources, we can reduce the disadvantages and help all students succeed under the new system.

💡 My Reflections and Notes

Write down key insights, teaching ideas, personal reflections, or any information you want to remember.

Chapter 05

College Admission System — Shaping Students, Shaping Society

Warm-Up

- What do you know about the CSAT (*Suneung*) and its role in university admissions in Korea?
- What is your opinion on the EBS-CSAT linkage system? Does it help or limit students?
- How does the pressure to enter a top university affect high school students' lives and choices?
- Do you think English education is shaped more by test preparation or communication goals?

Introduction

In the Republic of Korea, the college admission system is more than a gateway to higher education; it's a defining force in students' lives from an early age. At its center is the College Scholastic Ability Test (CSAT or *Suneung*), a high-stakes exam that determines not only university placement but also career paths, social status, and often family pride. The pressure leading up to this one-day test is immense, with many students sacrificing sleep, social life, and mental health to prepare.

A unique feature of Korea's admission system is its link to EBS, the public education broadcasting service. To reduce reliance on private education, the government designed the CSAT to align with EBS content. While intended to level the playing field, it has instead created a system where students focus narrowly on EBS materials, often at the expense of creativity, critical thinking, and genuine language use.

This test-driven culture shapes how English is taught in high schools. The CSAT English section emphasizes vocabulary, grammar, and reading comprehension over speaking or writing. As a result, many students master test strategies but lack real-world communicative skills. English becomes a subject to conquer, not a language to use, raising concerns about long-term effectiveness.

China's Gaokao is similar to Korea's CSAT: an intense, high-stakes exam that largely determines university access. In China, the pressure may be even greater, as university prestige deeply affects future employment and social mobility. By contrast, countries like the United States use a holistic admission system that evaluates students on multiple dimensions. American colleges consider GPA, standardized test scores, personal essays, recommendation letters, extracurricular activities, and sometimes interviews. The aim is to assess the whole student—their academic ability, personal character, and future potential. Although this system also has its flaws, it places greater value on individuality and well-rounded development.

This chapter explores the strengths and weaknesses of Korea's college admission system, especially its impact on English education. It also considers what educators can learn from other countries, and how teachers can better support students in this high-pressure environment—academically, emotionally, and ethically.

👤 Chitchat with Mates

1 If you could change one thing about the CSAT, what would it be and why?

	Answers
Me	
Mate 1	
Mate 2	
Mate 3	

2 Do you think preparing for the CSAT helped you improve your English skills in a meaningful way?

	Answers
Me	
Mate 1	
Mate 2	
Mate 3	

3 What differences have you noticed between English for tests and English for real communication?

	Answers
Me	
Mate 1	
Mate 2	
Mate 3	

4 How would you feel if Korea adopted a more holistic college admission system like in the U.S.?

	Answers
Me	
Mate 1	
Mate 2	
Mate 3	

 In-depth Reading

A System That Structures Student Lives

In the Republic of Korea, the college admission system is a defining force in the lives of students, families, and schools. More than a process for entering university, it reflects and reinforces the nation's cultural values, particularly those tied to academic achievement, competition, and national progress. At the core of this system are two main admission tracks: *susi* (early admission) and *jeongsi* (regular admission). While *jeongsi* is based primarily on the College Scholastic Ability Test, a high-stakes, one-day national exam, *susi* focuses on a combination of high school GPA, self-introduction essays, school activities, recommendation letters, and sometimes interviews. Students may pursue one or both routes, depending on their strengths and academic strategy.

Susi has grown in significance over the past decade. Today, over 70% of university admissions occur through this early admission track. Universities use it to select students who demonstrate potential beyond test scores. However, it is not less competitive. It requires years of strategic planning, including maintaining strong grades, compiling portfolios, and participating in extracurricular activities. *Jeongsi* appeals to students who may not have top GPAs but excel on standardized tests, especially the CSAT.

The CSAT includes sections on Korean, mathematics, English, and social studies and science subjects. Among these, English plays a central role, not only in the CSAT but also in university interviews, scholarships, and job qualifications. However, English education is shaped more by test preparation than by communicative goals. The exam-centric approach emphasizes reading comprehension, grammar drills, and vocabulary memorization. Many high school graduates can interpret complex texts but struggle to speak fluently, revealing a gap between academic performance and practical language ability.

EBS-CSAT Linkage: A Well-Intended but Narrowing Policy

To reduce dependence on private education, the Korean government implemented a policy linking CSAT content to EBS (Educational Broadcasting System) materials. This linkage was meant to increase fairness by allowing all students access to official test-aligned resources at little or no cost. However, the effect has been a narrowing of content and classroom focus. In English education, many students now prioritize memorizing EBS passages and practicing fixed problem types, limiting exposure to authentic or creative language tasks.

Teachers often feel compelled to tailor instruction to EBS content to help students perform well on the CSAT. As a result, classrooms increasingly rely on drilling practice questions and reviewing sample answers. While this may improve test scores, it often deepens the divide between what students can do on paper and how they use language in real situations.

Pressure Beyond the Exam Room

Whether students follow the *susi* or *jeongsi* route, their high school years are shaped by relentless preparation. *Susi* applicants must maintain consistently high GPAs, build activity portfolios, and prepare essays or interviews. *Jeongsi* applicants focus intensely on CSAT subjects, often attending private academies to gain a competitive edge. Both routes are demanding and offer no guarantees of admission.

The dual-track system influences how schools prioritize subjects, structure class time, and measure success. Students are frequently burdened by long hours of study, psychological pressure, and limited time for rest or personal development. Academic performance becomes central to students' self-worth, and university placement is often seen as a symbol of social status.

Moreover, the early deadlines of *susi* applications typically submitted in the early fall of senior year mean students must balance portfolio preparation and academic performance simultaneously. This can lead to exhaustion and emotional burnout, especially for students in highly competitive environments.

Global Comparisons: China and the United Kingdom

While Korea is not alone in using high-stakes exams for university entry, comparisons with other systems reveal different values. In China, the Gaokao serves as the primary path to higher education. Like the CSAT, it tests subjects such as Chinese, mathematics, English, and electives in science or humanities. The Gaokao spans two to three days and is regarded as the most critical moment in a student's academic life. The exam is not uniform across the entire country. While the core subjects are similar, the content and standards of the exam can vary by province.

Before the Gaokao, each university, especially the top-tier universities, is allocated a specific number of enrollment quotas for each province. This means that a university might be allowed to admit, for example, 100 students from

Beijing, 50 from Henan, and 20 from Tibet. This regional quota system favors students in cities like Beijing and Shanghai by setting lower cut-off scores for elite universities. In contrast, rural students often need higher scores to access the same opportunities. The Gaokao remains almost entirely exam-based, with little consideration of student background, personality, or non-academic accomplishments.

In the United Kingdom, admission relies on a combination of academic results and holistic components. Students are offered places primarily based on predicted or actual A-level results, which are subject-specific exams taken at the end of secondary school. They must also submit a personal statement and a teacher reference through the UCAS (Universities and Colleges Admissions Service) platform. This system allows students to explain their motivations and subject interests and provides room for showcasing personal experiences beyond the classroom.

At competitive institutions such as Oxford and Cambridge, applicants may also be required to take university-specific entrance tests and attend interviews. These elements aim to assess intellectual curiosity and academic potential. While the UK model still centers on academic merit, the use of personal narratives and face-to-face interaction reflects a broader view of student ability. However, critics point out that students from private or well-funded schools often receive more support with application materials and interview preparation, raising concerns about equal access.

Conclusion: Admissions as a Reflection of National Values

Korea's dual-track system—*susi* and *jeongsi*—continues to shape not only student learning but the entire structure of secondary education. Though the system attempts to diversify the way students are assessed, both tracks remain competitive and demanding. Policies like the EBS-CSAT linkage and the expansion of holistic elements in early admissions were introduced to enhance equity, yet they have also led to rigid classroom routines and long-term academic pressure.

Comparing Korea with China and the United Kingdom illustrates how admission systems reflect deeper cultural beliefs about merit, fairness, and success. Korea places heavy value on both exam achievement and academic consistency. China emphasizes exam excellence almost exclusively. The UK takes a more balanced approach, blending academic outcomes with character-based evaluations. Each model has strengths and drawbacks, but all reveal how college admissions serve not just to sort students, but to express what a society values in its future citizens.

In Korea, university entrance remains a crucial rite of passage. As the competition grows and societal expectations remain high, understanding the mechanics and effects of both *susi* and *jeongsi* is essential for improving educational equity and aligning English education with broader, real-world needs.

Comprehension Questions

1 What are the main differences between the *susi* and *jeongsi* systems in Korea, and how do they shape students' academic strategies?

2 How has the EBS-CSAT linkage policy influenced the way English is taught and learned in Korean high schools?

3 What are some of the emotional and academic pressures students face when preparing for both the *susi* and *jeongsi* admission routes?

4 How does China's Gaokao differ from Korea's CSAT in terms of structure, fairness, and reliance on test scores?

5 In what ways does the UK's university admission system attempt to assess student potential beyond academic exam results?

 **Ask AI**

Is it competitive to get into college in <u>Singapore</u>? Why or why not?

❓ In-depth Discussion Questions

1 How does the dual-track system of *susi* and *jeongsi* affect students' priorities in high school? Does it offer flexibility or simply extend academic pressure across more years?

2 In what ways does focusing on EBS materials for CSAT preparation limit students' real-life English communication skills? Should English classes be restructured to balance exams and language use?

3 The *susi* system favors students with stronger school records and support. What strategies or policy changes could make this route more accessible to students from disadvantaged backgrounds?

4 Did your high school experience prepare you for *susi*-style applications? What support or resources could schools offer to help students build competitive academic and extracurricular records?

5 Is relying on a single high-stakes test like the CSAT a fair way to determine university admission? What are the advantages and risks of this kind of evaluation system?

6 Could Korea realistically require personal statements and interviews in university admissions, as seen in the UK? What safeguards would be needed to prevent new forms of inequality?

7 What lessons can Korea learn from China's Gaokao system, especially regarding regional inequality and intense exam pressure? Could aspects of the Gaokao inform changes to the CSAT?

8 Why is there such strong social pressure to enter top universities in Korea? How might shifting cultural views on college prestige reduce stress and broaden student goals?

9 Make a discussion question based on the information you have obtained for "Ask AI."

⦿ Debate

1 *Susi* admission increases inequality and should be replaced with a more standardized system like *jeongsi*. (Focus: fairness vs. holistic evaluation)

Agree	Disagree

2 The CSAT should include a speaking and writing section to reflect real English communication skills. (Focus: test practicality vs. language relevance)

Agree	Disagree

3 The CSAT should be offered two or three times a year instead of only once. (Focus: consistency and fairness vs. increased pressure and logistical challenges)

Agree	Disagree

4 Korea should adopt a more holistic college admission model similar to the U.K. or the U.S. (Focus: cultural fit vs. global standards)

Agree	Disagree

ⓘ Wrap-Up: Your Turn to Write

Prompt: *Reflect on the strengths and weaknesses of Korea's college admission system. Based on your experience and goals as a teacher, what changes or improvements would you like to see?*

Sample Essay

Korea's college admission system plays a major role in shaping students' academic lives, and while it offers structure and standards, I believe it needs important changes. The dual-track approach—*susi* and *jeongsi*—provides students with options, but in reality, both paths are highly competitive and stressful. As a high school student, I remember classmates building portfolios from their first year, while others poured all their energy into CSAT prep. Neither path felt flexible or humane. The intense focus on competition often left students burned out before graduation.

One problem is the overemphasis on test performance. In particular, English education becomes about solving CSAT questions rather than learning how to communicate. Students who can answer reading comprehension questions may still feel nervous speaking in real situations. Also, the EBS-linked study narrows students' focus to patterns and memorization, leaving little room for creativity or independent thinking. Instead of fostering curiosity, this system encourages students to follow models and templates.

As a future teacher, I hope to help students see English as a tool for connection, not just a subject to master for exams. I also believe the college admission system should be more balanced. Offering the CSAT more than once a year, increasing interview-based admission, or expanding diverse evaluation methods could help relieve pressure and recognize a wider range of student talents. Including more project-based or discussion-based assessments may also highlight strengths not visible in test scores.

The current system pushes students to work hard, but it also creates high anxiety and inequality. Students from well-off families often receive more support through tutoring and consulting, while others struggle to keep up. I believe a healthier, fairer system is possible—one that values both academic performance and personal growth, and prepares students for life beyond exams.

💡 My Reflections and Notes

Write down key insights, teaching ideas, personal reflections, or any information you want to remember.

Chapter 06

Who Owns the Classroom? —
Rights, Authority, and Responsibility in School Life

Warm-Up

- Have you ever witnessed a conflict between a teacher and a student in school?
- What do you think are the most important rights students should have in school?
- Should teachers be strict to maintain discipline, or friendly to build trust?
- How much influence should parents have on what happens in a teacher's classroom?

Introduction

In recent years, debates over student rights, teacher authority, and parental involvement have grown louder in South Korea. Once a place where the teacher's word was final, today's classroom has become a contested space, where students, parents, and teachers all assert their roles and expectations. Schools are no longer just places for instruction; they are arenas of negotiation between rights and responsibilities, where social values, legal awareness, and generational differences all collide.

Students today are more aware of their legal and human rights, and many schools now have student councils, feedback channels, and complaint systems to protect learners from unfair treatment. While this is a positive step toward a more democratic and accountable education system, it also creates new challenges. Teachers may hesitate to discipline students or enforce rules, fearing backlash or formal complaints from parents or education offices. This shift in the balance of power has led to a growing sense of uncertainty among educators about how much authority they actually have in the classroom.

At the same time, parental involvement in education has expanded significantly. In the name of advocacy and concern, some parents demand greater say in school policies, class activities, and even teaching styles. While healthy cooperation between home and school can support student learning, excessive interference can undermine a teacher's professional judgment, lower classroom morale, and disrupt the overall learning environment for everyone involved.

As a result, many teachers struggle to maintain effective classroom management while respecting student rights and balancing parental expectations. The boundaries between care, control, and authority are becoming increasingly blurred, leaving room for conflict and confusion.

This chapter explores the complex dynamics of ownership and authority in the classroom. Who sets the tone for behavior and learning? What rights and responsibilities do students, teachers, and parents each hold? And how can schools create an environment where mutual respect, student voice, and educational integrity coexist in harmony?

👤 Chitchat with Mates

1 What would you do if a classmate refused to follow a teacher's instructions?

	Answers
Me	
Mate 1	
Mate 2	
Mate 3	

2 Do you think students should be allowed to record lessons or complain about teachers online?

	Answers
Me	
Mate 1	
Mate 2	
Mate 3	

3 What's the best way for a teacher to earn students' respect?

	Answers
Me	
Mate 1	
Mate 2	
Mate 3	

4 How would you feel if your parent contacted your professor without telling you in regard to your study?

	Answers
Me	
Mate 1	
Mate 2	
Mate 3	

📖 In-depth Reading

A Shift in the Classroom

In today's Korean schools, the classroom is no longer a space governed solely by the teacher's voice. Once considered the unquestioned authority, teachers now share that space with increasingly vocal students and highly involved parents. This shift has triggered a broader conversation about the rights, responsibilities, and limits of each stakeholder in education. As students grow more aware of their legal protections, and as parents take a more active role in shaping school decisions, the classroom has transformed into a site of negotiation and, sometimes, tension.

South Korea's movement toward protecting student rights has been both empowering and controversial. In response to past incidents of abuse and excessive discipline, many regional education offices now encourage schools to adopt student charters, ban corporal punishment, and establish channels for students to express concerns. In some schools, students are involved in decision-making committees, and have platforms to voice their opinions on rules, schedules, and even teacher evaluations.

This empowerment is a welcome change for those who believe schools should reflect democratic values. However, it has also created challenges for classroom management. Some teachers report hesitation in enforcing discipline out of fear that students may record incidents or file formal complaints. Others express concern that the line between protecting rights and challenging authority is becoming increasingly difficult to navigate.

Teacher Authority Under Pressure

Traditionally, Korean teachers were respected as moral and academic guides. Their authority in the classroom was rarely questioned. Today, however, that respect is more conditional. Teachers are expected not only to deliver instruction but also to meet students' emotional needs, respond to parental concerns, and document their every action.

This expanded responsibility often comes with limited institutional support. When conflicts arise, schools may prioritize parental satisfaction or public image over teacher autonomy. As a result, many teachers feel their authority has weakened, making it harder to manage disruptive behavior or maintain consistent discipline. Veteran teachers sometimes describe a feeling of walking on eggshells, unsure if their professional judgment will be supported by administrators or challenged by parents.

Parental Involvement: Support or Overstep?

Parental involvement is crucial in any education system. When done constructively, it fosters better academic outcomes and stronger emotional support for students. In Korea, however, parental engagement often extends far beyond homework help or school events. Some parents regularly contact teachers about grades, homework policies, or classroom discipline and expect immediate responses.

While some involvement is beneficial, over-involvement can have damaging effects. Teachers may feel pressured to change their classroom practices to appease certain parents. In extreme cases, parental complaints have led to public criticism or administrative reprimands of teachers. This environment can discourage innovation and erode the trust that teachers need to create positive learning spaces.

Classroom Management in a Changing Landscape

With student rights expanding and parental voices growing louder, classroom management has become a delicate balancing act. The teacher must maintain order and engagement while respecting student autonomy and managing external expectations. Strategies that once worked—authoritative discipline, strict seating plans, or confiscation of devices—may now lead to conflict or backlash.

To adapt, many teachers are turning to relationship-based management approaches: setting shared expectations, involving students in rule-making, and creating a climate of mutual respect. While these methods often result in deeper engagement and fewer behavioral problems, they also require time, energy, and consistency. Not every teacher feels equipped or supported to implement them effectively, especially in large classes with diverse needs. Furthermore, inconsistent policies between schools or lack of administrative backing can discourage even the most committed educators from adopting these progressive approaches.

Institutional Roles and Policy Gaps

While teachers are at the frontline, the larger education system plays a critical role in shaping classroom dynamics. Schools, principals, and education offices set policies that define how much autonomy teachers have and how conflicts are resolved. Yet many teachers argue that current systems do not provide enough clarity or protection. Guidelines are often vague, and procedures for handling disputes with students or parents are inconsistent across schools.

There is also a lack of training in legal literacy and conflict resolution for teachers. Most educators enter the profession with strong subject knowledge but limited preparation in managing complex human dynamics. This gap leaves them vulnerable when issues arise and contributes to the growing stress and burnout reported across the profession. Without a clear framework or adequate institutional backing, even experienced teachers may feel powerless or unsupported, especially when dealing with controversial or emotionally charged situations that require careful judgment and diplomacy.

Toward a Balanced Classroom Culture

So how can Korean classrooms evolve into spaces where rights, authority, and responsibility coexist? First, clear boundaries and shared values must be reestablished. Students should understand that having rights does not eliminate responsibilities. Teachers need reaffirmation of their professional autonomy and a support system that backs fair, reasonable decisions.

Second, schools must create consistent systems for communication and conflict resolution. This includes standardized procedures for handling complaints, transparent discipline policies, and regular dialogue between teachers, students, and parents. Such systems reduce misunderstandings and ensure that all voices are heard without any single group dominating.

Finally, teacher training programs must evolve. In addition to pedagogy and content knowledge, future teachers need preparation in legal rights, emotional intelligence, communication strategies, and parental engagement. Equipping teachers with these tools can reduce fear, increase confidence, and promote healthier classroom environments.

Conclusion: Shared Ownership, Shared Responsibility

The question of who owns the classroom has no simple answer. In truth, it is a shared space, a place where students learn, teachers lead, and parents support. Each group plays a vital role, but balance is key. Without it, respect breaks down, roles blur, and the educational mission suffers. The future of Korean education depends not on restoring old hierarchies but on building new partnerships—ones based on trust, respect, and mutual responsibility. By clarifying roles, improving communication, and providing stronger institutional support, schools can become environments where everyone feels heard, valued, and empowered to contribute.

Comprehension Questions

1 What are some examples of how student rights have expanded in Korean schools in recent years?

2 How has teacher authority changed, and what are some consequences of this shift?

3 In what ways can excessive parental involvement negatively impact classroom dynamics?

4 What challenges do teachers face when trying to implement relationship-based classroom management?

5 What are three key recommendations for building a more balanced classroom culture?

Ask AI

How are teacher rights protected in Finland?

In-depth Discussion Questions

1 How can schools balance protecting student rights with allowing teachers to maintain classroom authority? Should one take priority when the two conflict?

2 What kind of support or training should teachers receive to handle conflicts with students and parents more effectively?

3 At what point does parental involvement cross the line into classroom interference? How can schools set healthy boundaries without alienating parents?

4 Do you think Korean schools should have national-level policies that clearly define student, teacher, and parent responsibilities? Why or why not?

_____
_____
_____
_____
_____
_____

5 What role should students play in shaping classroom rules or school policy? Can student voice be part of classroom management without weakening teacher authority?

_____
_____
_____
_____
_____
_____

6 In what ways could schools ensure that teachers feel professionally respected and protected when disputes arise?

_____
_____
_____
_____
_____
_____

7 How can communication between teachers and parents be improved to avoid misunderstandings or escalation of minor issues?

_____
_____
_____
_____
_____
_____

8 What would an ideal classroom look like in terms of rights, responsibilities, discipline, and mutual respect? Describe the balance you would want to see.

_____
_____
_____
_____
_____
_____

9 Make a discussion question based on the information you have obtained for "Ask AI."

_____
_____
_____
_____
_____
_____

🎙 Debate

1 Students should have equal decision-making power as teachers in setting classroom rules and policies. (Focus: democratic participation vs. teacher expertise and classroom order)

Agree	Disagree

2 Teachers should not be required to respond to parental concerns outside of school hours. (Focus: work-life balance for teachers vs. parental right to engagement)

Agree	Disagree

3 Recording or documenting teacher behavior in class should be banned without explicit consent. (Focus: teacher privacy and authority vs. student protection and transparency)

Agree	Disagree

4 Parental complaints or suggestions should not directly influence how teachers conduct their classes. (Focus: professional autonomy vs. parental involvement in a child's education)

Agree	Disagree

ⓘ Wrap-Up: Your Turn to Write

Prompt: *What kind of classroom environment do you believe is best for learning, and how should responsibilities be shared among students, teachers, and parents?*

Sample Essay

After reading about the current challenges in Korean classrooms, I've realized how complex the balance between student rights, teacher authority, and parental involvement has become. While I support students being treated with fairness and respect, I also believe that too much focus on student rights without clear responsibilities can lead to classroom disorder and confusion.

Teachers should be trusted as professionals. If students or parents constantly question their every decision, it becomes difficult to teach effectively. However, I also think teachers need to listen to students and build relationships based on trust rather than control. A classroom should not feel like a battlefield between freedom and discipline.

Parents play a crucial role, but they should act as supporters, not supervisors. When parents interfere too much with how teachers run their classes, it sends the wrong message to students. It can also damage the teacher's confidence and authority in front of the class. At the same time, schools should welcome parental voices when approached respectfully, especially when they support student well-being or learning.

The ideal classroom is one where everyone has a voice but also understands their role. Students should feel safe to express opinions, teachers should feel empowered to lead, and parents should communicate with respect and boundaries. Schools also need clear policies to support teachers when conflicts arise. In the end, a successful learning environment is based on mutual trust, active communication, and shared responsibility among all members of the school community.

⊙ My Reflections and Notes

Write down key insights, teaching ideas, personal reflections, or any information you want to remember.

Chapter 07

Welcoming Diversity — Multicultural Education in Korean Classrooms

Warm-Up

- Have you ever had a classmate or friend from a multicultural background?
- What comes to your mind when you hear the word "multicultural"?
- Do you think Korean society is welcoming to people from different cultures?
- What challenges might students face if their parents don't speak Korean?

Introduction

Korea, once considered an ethnically and culturally homogeneous society, is rapidly becoming more diverse. In the past two decades, the number of multicultural families in Korea has increased significantly, driven by international marriages, immigration, and labor migration. As a result, more children from multicultural backgrounds are entering the Korean school system. These students bring rich cultural experiences, new languages, and different perspectives, but they also face serious challenges in adjusting to Korean society and education.

One major issue is language. Many children in multicultural families grow up in homes where Korean is not the primary language. This language barrier can make it difficult for them to follow lessons, interact with peers, and express themselves confidently in school settings. Some fall behind academically simply because they cannot fully understand classroom instructions or textbooks.

Another concern is discrimination and peer pressure. Despite improvements in public awareness, many multicultural students still experience bullying, exclusion, or insensitive remarks from classmates or even teachers. This can lead to low self-esteem, social withdrawal, and emotional distress. Combined with language and cultural differences, these social challenges often result in lower academic performance among multicultural students compared to their Korean peers.

However, these difficulties are not unresolvable. With proper support such as Korean language education, emotional counseling, inclusive teaching practices, and multicultural awareness programs, schools can become more welcoming environments. Teachers play a crucial role in creating inclusive classrooms that respect and celebrate diversity, rather than suppressing it.

As Korea continues to change, so must its approach to education. In this chapter, we will explore how multiculturalism is shaping Korean schools, the problems it brings, and the solutions needed to build a more inclusive and supportive system for all students, regardless of background.

😊 Chitchat with Mates

1 Do you think it's easy or difficult for a child to grow up in Korea without speaking Korean at home? Explain your answer.

	Answers
Me	
Mate 1	
Mate 2	
Mate 3	

2 Have you ever seen someone treated unfairly because they looked or spoke differently? Describe the situation.

	Answers
Me	
Mate 1	
Mate 2	
Mate 3	

3 What cultural differences have you noticed between Korean and foreign friends or classmates?

	Answers
Me	
Mate 1	
Mate 2	
Mate 3	

4 Should Korean schools teach students more about world cultures and diversity? Why or why not?

	Answers
Me	
Mate 1	
Mate 2	
Mate 3	

In-depth Reading

Demographic Shifts in Korea

Not long ago, Korea was considered one of the most ethnically homogeneous countries in the world. The idea of a "pure-blooded" national identity shaped its culture, politics, and education for generations. But over the past two decades, this narrative has rapidly changed. Korea is no longer monocultural. The number of multicultural families formed through international marriages, foreign workers, and migrant communities, has grown dramatically, especially in rural areas and among younger generations. As a result, Korean classrooms are becoming more diverse, both linguistically and culturally. With these changes come new opportunities, but also new challenges.

According to recent statistics, more than 180,000 students in Korea come from multicultural families, and this number continues to rise. Many of these children have one Korean parent and one foreign-born parent, often from countries like Vietnam, China, the Philippines, or Central Asia. Others are born abroad and move to Korea at a young age. While these students bring unique strengths such as multilingual skills and diverse worldviews, they also often face structural barriers within the school system.

One of the most serious issues is language. Children from multicultural families often grow up speaking a language other than Korean at home, or in homes where Korean is spoken with limited fluency. This creates challenges not just in everyday conversation, but in reading textbooks, writing essays, and understanding class discussions. Without strong Korean language support, many students fall behind academically, not because of a lack of intelligence or effort, but because of communication difficulties.

Language, Culture, and Identity

Language barriers are deeply tied to a student's confidence and sense of belonging. A student who cannot follow the teacher's instructions or express ideas clearly may begin to feel isolated or ashamed. These emotional responses often go unnoticed in a classroom focused mainly on test scores and speed. Moreover, these students may be hesitant to speak up in class or ask for help, which can further reduce participation and performance. Over time, this silence may be misinterpreted as disinterest or low ability, reinforcing negative stereotypes and lowering expectations.

Cultural differences also play a major role. Many students from multicultural families feel pressure to "act Korean" and suppress aspects of their heritage in order to fit in. School events, classroom norms, food customs, and even group behavior are often based on unspoken Korean traditions that may confuse or alienate newcomers. The language of inclusion is often missing, and students quickly learn that "blending in" is rewarded more than expressing difference. Instead of being celebrated for their diversity, these students are often expected to assimilate quickly, sometimes at the cost of losing touch with their cultural roots. This struggle between adapting and maintaining one's identity can lead to emotional exhaustion and internal conflict, especially for young learners trying to understand who they are.

Discrimination and Peer Pressure

Although Korean society has become more open to diversity, many multicultural students still experience discrimination. Some are teased or bullied for their appearance, accents, or foreign-sounding names. Teachers may unconsciously lower expectations for them or fail to intervene when hurtful comments are made. These microaggressions accumulate over time and can lead to long-term emotional and academic problems. Studies have shown that multicultural students are at a higher risk for school dropout, depression, and low self-esteem.

Peer pressure can also be intense. In group-centered Korean classrooms, being "different" often makes it harder to be included. A child who brings different food for lunch, struggles with Korean, or doesn't understand a local idiom may be excluded, even unintentionally. The desire to belong may lead students to hide or feel ashamed of their cultural identity. Over time, this can create a sense of inner conflict, where students feel they must choose between their background and fitting in.

Academic Performance and Systemic Gaps

The challenges mentioned above often result in lower academic performance among multicultural students compared to their peers. Language delays, limited parental support, and social isolation all contribute to this gap. Additionally, many parents in multicultural families face economic hardships and may not have the time, knowledge, or language skills to support their children's education. In rural areas, where international marriages are more common, schools often lack trained staff or adequate resources to provide the support these students need.

Despite government efforts to improve the situation, such as offering Korean language classes, multicultural support centers, and teacher training, gaps remain. Many initiatives are temporary, underfunded, or inconsistently implemented across regions. A nationwide, integrated approach to multicultural education is still lacking.

Toward Inclusive and Supportive Schools

So what can be done? First, schools must recognize that multicultural education is not just for "foreign" students—it is for all students. A truly multicultural curriculum exposes everyone to global perspectives, different languages, and diverse histories. Teachers should include materials that reflect a variety of cultures and encourage open discussions about identity and belonging. Classrooms that normalize difference create an environment where all students can thrive.

Second, Korean language support must be strengthened and sustained. It is not enough to offer short-term language classes. Multicultural students may need several years of structured, age-appropriate Korean education to catch up and succeed. Teachers should also be trained in how to differentiate instruction and support language learners in mainstream classes.

Third, schools must actively fight discrimination by promoting empathy and cultural understanding. Peer mentoring programs, multicultural awareness days, and inclusive classroom policies can reduce bullying and help students build friendships across cultural lines. Teachers must lead by example, showing respect for all backgrounds and correcting prejudice when it arises.

Finally, parental involvement should be expanded. Schools can offer Korean classes for immigrant parents, translation services, and community events that welcome families from different backgrounds. When parents feel respected and involved, they are more likely to support their children's education and build trust with teachers.

The Role of Future Teachers

For future teachers, multicultural education is not an optional topic. It is an essential part of your role. As Korea continues to diversify, classrooms will increasingly reflect a range of languages, beliefs, and backgrounds. Being a teacher in this environment means being not only an educator, but also a guide, an advocate, and a bridge between cultures. You must learn to see difference not as a problem to fix, but as a strength to embrace. With patience, empathy, and skill, you can help build a more inclusive and fair school system—one where all students, regardless of origin, feel they belong.

🔍 Comprehension Questions

1. What is one of the main reasons multicultural students fall behind academically in Korea?

2. How can cultural differences affect a student's sense of belonging in school?

3. What are some examples of discrimination that multicultural students may face?

4. Why is peer pressure especially difficult for students from multicultural backgrounds?

5. What roles can teachers play in making schools more inclusive for all students?

 **Ask AI**

Show key statistics in regard to multicultural education in Australia.

❓ In-depth Discussion Questions

1 How can Korean teachers create inclusive classrooms that celebrate cultural diversity while still maintaining a shared sense of community among students from different language and cultural backgrounds?

2 In what ways does the pressure to "act Korean" affect the identity development of multicultural students, and how can educators support both adaptation and cultural pride?

3 What specific strategies can teachers use to support students who struggle with Korean language skills, without making them feel singled out or less capable than their peers?

4 How can schools balance the need to teach Korean culture and values with respect for students' diverse home cultures, especially during national holidays or school events?

_____
_____
_____
_____
_____
_____

5 What role should Korean classmates play in supporting their multicultural peers, and how can teachers encourage empathy and reduce social exclusion or bullying?

_____
_____
_____
_____
_____
_____

6 How can Korean language education for immigrant parents positively influence their children's academic success and emotional well-being, and what support systems should schools provide?

_____
_____
_____
_____
_____
_____

7 In what ways does standardized testing disadvantage multicultural students, and how can assessment methods be redesigned to better reflect diverse learners' abilities and progress?

8 Should multicultural education be a mandatory part of teacher training in Korea? Why or why not, and what core competencies should future teachers develop to teach in diverse classrooms?

9 Make a discussion question based on the information you have obtained for "Ask AI."

💬 Debate

1 Korean schools should provide separate Korean language classes for multicultural students instead of integrating them immediately into regular classrooms. (Focus: tailored language support vs. full social integration from the beginning)

Agree	Disagree

2 Teachers should receive mandatory multicultural training as part of their teacher certification process. (Focus: standardized teacher preparation vs. teacher freedom and individual judgment)

Agree	Disagree

3 Schools should actively celebrate students' cultural backgrounds through events, food, and language days. (Focus: cultural expression and inclusion vs. risk of tokenism or distraction from academics)

Agree	Disagree

4 Multicultural students should receive extra support on national exams due to linguistic and cultural disadvantages. (Focus: equity and fairness vs. equal standards and merit-based assessment)

Agree	Disagree

ⓘ Wrap-Up: Your Turn to Write

Prompt: *What can Korean teachers do to help multicultural students succeed academically and feel accepted socially in school? Describe one or two practical strategies and explain why they are important.*

Sample Essay

I believe one of the most important things Korean teachers can do to support multicultural students is to create a classroom environment where all students feel valued and safe. Many multicultural students struggle not only with language but also with identity, especially if their appearance, name, or home culture is different from their classmates'. Teachers need to recognize these challenges and actively build a culture of inclusion.

One practical strategy is to include multicultural content in everyday lessons. For example, when teaching about world history or literature, teachers can introduce stories or figures from countries that reflect the backgrounds of their students. This sends a message that diversity is normal and valuable, not something to hide or feel ashamed of. It also helps Korean students learn to appreciate different cultures, which can reduce bullying and stereotypes.

Another helpful strategy is pairing multicultural students with peer mentors. A Korean-speaking classmate who is kind and patient can help the student feel less alone, especially in the early months. Teachers can rotate partners or form study groups that mix students from different backgrounds. This encourages friendships and mutual understanding.

These small changes can make a big difference. When students feel accepted, they are more willing to speak, ask questions, and participate in class. That's the first step to academic improvement. As a future teacher, I want to be someone who notices the quiet students and makes sure they're not left behind, especially if they come from multicultural families. Helping them succeed is not only fair, but also necessary for Korea's future as a more global and inclusive society.

⊙ My Reflections and Notes

Write down key insights, teaching ideas, personal reflections, or any information you want to remember.

Chapter 08

Learning Without Limits — Education for Students with Special Needs

Warm-Up

- Have you ever had a classmate with a learning or developmental disability?
- What comes to mind when you hear the term "special needs student"?
- Do you think students with special needs should be in the same classroom as other students? Why or why not?
- What kind of support do you think schools need to provide for students with ADHD or autism?

Introduction

Modern education aims to be inclusive, valuing diversity and ensuring that every student receives the support they need to succeed. However, for students with special needs such as autism spectrum disorder, ADHD, learning disabilities, intellectual disabilities, or emotional and behavioral disorders, this goal often remains out of reach.

In South Korea, students with special needs make up a growing but still often overlooked part of the education system. These students may face challenges in communication, concentration, emotional control, or academic processing. For instance, dyslexia can make reading a daily struggle, while ADHD can affect focus and classroom behavior. Other students, such as those with Down syndrome or intellectual disabilities, may require specialized instruction and more individualized attention. Despite the legal framework supporting special education, the actual accommodations available in public schools are often limited. Many teachers lack training in special education, and schools may not have the resources to provide aides, assistive technologies, or tailored programs.

One major debate is whether students with special needs should be placed in regular classrooms (inclusive education) or taught in separate special schools or classes. Inclusion helps normalize difference and promotes empathy, but without proper support, both the students with disabilities and their peers can struggle. Teachers may feel overwhelmed, and special needs students may face bullying or isolation.

Korean society is gradually changing its view on disabilities, but stigma and misunderstanding still exist. Psychological conditions such as anxiety, depression, or trauma-related disorders are especially under-discussed, though they deeply affect learning and classroom behavior. Schools are beginning to introduce more mental health support, but gaps remain.

Creating a truly inclusive education system requires more than integration; it demands understanding, training, resources, and compassion. This chapter examines the current situation and future possibilities for students with special needs, challenging readers to think deeply about what fairness and success mean in education.

👤 Chitchat with Mates

1 Do you think our school is inclusive to students with different learning needs? Why or why not?

	Answers
Me	
Mate 1	
Mate 2	
Mate 3	

2 What do you know about disorders like dyslexia or ADHD in class?

	Answers
Me	
Mate 1	
Mate 2	
Mate 3	

3 If your class had a student with autism, how would you want your teacher to support them?

	Answers
Me	
Mate 1	
Mate 2	
Mate 3	

4 What can students do to help create a more supportive classroom for everyone?

	Answers
Me	
Mate 1	
Mate 2	
Mate 3	

📖 In-depth Reading

Students with Special Needs

Education is a fundamental human right, and every child, regardless of their physical, intellectual, emotional, or behavioral condition, deserves an opportunity to learn and grow in an environment that respects their needs. However, students with special needs often face complex barriers in education systems, including insufficient resources, lack of trained staff, social stigma, and questions about where and how they should be educated. As societies strive toward inclusiveness, the education of students with disabilities and learning differences is becoming an urgent issue, not only in South Korea but around the world.

Special needs education covers a broad spectrum of conditions. These include autism spectrum disorder (ASD), attention-deficit/ hyperactivity disorder (ADHD), learning disabilities such as dyslexia (reading), dyscalculia (math), and dysgraphia (writing), intellectual disabilities, Down syndrome, emotional and behavioral disorders, and various psychological conditions. Some students may function at or near the intellectual level of their peers but require specialized teaching strategies. Others may need long-term support and individualized education programs (IEPs) tailored to their developmental level.

Understanding the Needs and Types of Support

The needs of students with disabilities are as diverse as the students themselves. For example, a student with dyslexia may have average or above-average intelligence but find reading extremely difficult. A child with ADHD might struggle to sit still or concentrate during class, even though they are curious and enthusiastic learners. An autistic student might be highly skilled in certain areas but experience difficulties in communication and social interaction.

The goal of special needs education is not to label or isolate students but to empower them with the tools and support they need to thrive. This might include providing assistive technologies, hiring teaching assistants, modifying classroom environments, or adjusting assessment methods. Emotional and psychological support is also crucial, especially for students with trauma histories, depression, or anxiety disorders. Without adequate care and understanding, these students can become disengaged, misunderstood, or even punished for behaviors stemming from their condition.

Inclusion vs. Segregation: The Ongoing Debate

One of the central questions in special needs education is whether students with disabilities should be integrated into regular classrooms or taught in separate settings. Inclusive education promotes learning alongside peers, which can foster empathy, reduce stigma, and provide equal access to curriculum. This approach is based on the principle that the problem lies not within the student, but in how the environment responds to their needs. A well-supported inclusive classroom can benefit all students by promoting diversity, tolerance, and differentiated instruction.

However, inclusion without adequate preparation can cause unintended harm. Teachers may feel overwhelmed by the diverse needs in one classroom, especially if they lack training in special education. Students with disabilities may feel isolated or bullied, while their classmates may feel confused or distracted. For inclusion to succeed, schools need sufficient resources, professional development, and a collaborative school culture that views differences as strengths rather than burdens.

On the other hand, special education schools or separate classrooms can offer individualized support and tailored instruction. These settings often have trained staff and smaller class sizes. Yet, they may also reinforce social exclusion and limit the opportunities for students with special needs to interact with peers without disabilities. The best solution may lie in a flexible, case-by-case approach that respects both the right to inclusion and the need for personalized education.

The Korean Context: Progress and Limitations

In South Korea, the government has taken steps toward promoting inclusive education, such as passing the Act on Special Education for Persons with Disabilities (장애인 등에 대한 특수교육법) and encouraging the integration of students with disabilities into mainstream schools. However, challenges remain. Special education teachers are in short supply, and many general education teachers receive limited training in how to support students with special needs. Some schools lack accessible facilities, appropriate materials, or counseling services.

Social stigma remains a major obstacle. Families of children with disabilities often face judgment, misunderstanding, or even discrimination. There have been cases of local residents opposing the construction of special schools in their neighborhoods, fearing that property values will drop or that their children's education will be disrupted. This resistance reflects a broader societal discomfort with disability, which must be addressed through awareness, empathy-building, and public education campaigns.

Another concern is the under-identification of students with "invisible" disabilities—those with psychological or learning disorders that are not immediately obvious. These students may quietly struggle for years without diagnosis or support. For instance, students with borderline IQ or mild dyslexia may fall through the cracks in a system that focuses heavily on standardized testing. The pressure to conform and compete can make their school life extremely stressful and demoralizing.

Looking Forward: Building an Inclusive and Compassionate System

To move forward, Korea, and other countries, must embrace a broader definition of student success. Education should not only focus on academic scores but also on social development, emotional resilience, and individual growth. A multi-tiered system of support can help address diverse needs. This includes universal design for learning (UDL), individualized education plans (IEPs), early screening, parent-teacher collaboration, and stronger mental health services.

Teacher education programs must include mandatory training in special education and inclusive practices. General education teachers need to understand how to modify instruction, manage inclusive classrooms, and recognize the signs of learning and emotional difficulties. Co-teaching models, where a general education teacher and a special educator collaborate in the same classroom, can be highly effective.

Schools also need to cultivate a more inclusive culture. This involves promoting kindness, peer support programs, anti-bullying campaigns, and a recognition that differences enrich the learning environment. When students learn to accept and support each other, the whole school community benefits.

Furthermore, policies must be backed by adequate funding. This includes budgets for special educators, accessible materials, mental health professionals, and community outreach. Governments and local authorities must view these investments not as charity but as essential steps toward educational equity.

The education of students with special needs is not just an educational issue; it is a *moral* one. It asks us whether we truly believe in equal opportunity, diversity, and human dignity. While many obstacles remain, there is also great potential for transformation. By embracing inclusive values, increasing support and training, and changing public perceptions, schools can become places where every student feels seen, supported, and capable of learning. A more inclusive education system is not only possible; it is necessary for a just and compassionate society.

🔍 Comprehension Questions

1 What are some examples of conditions included under the umbrella of special needs in education?

2 What are the pros and cons of inclusive education mentioned in the essay?

3 What challenges does the South Korean education system face in supporting students with special needs?

4 Why is teacher training important in building an inclusive classroom environment?

5 According to the essay, how should society change its perception of students with special needs?

 **Ask AI**

How do schools help students with special needs in the United States?

❓ In-depth Discussion Questions

1 What kinds of teacher training or professional development do you think are necessary to support students with autism, ADHD, or learning disabilities in regular classrooms?

___

2 How can schools balance the needs of students with special needs while still maintaining academic standards and classroom management for the entire class?

___

3 In what ways might inclusive education benefit not only students with special needs but also students without disabilities in terms of empathy, cooperation, and social awareness?

___

4 What are some reasons communities oppose building special education schools nearby, and how might these objections be addressed through policy or education campaigns?

_____
_____
_____
_____
_____
_____

5 How can schools provide effective emotional and psychological support for students with invisible disabilities, such as anxiety disorders or trauma-related behavioral problems?

_____
_____
_____
_____
_____
_____

6 What role should parents and guardians play in advocating for or participating in their children's special education plans, and what happens when that support is lacking?

_____
_____
_____
_____
_____
_____

7 What role should parents and guardians play in advocating for or participating in their children's special education plans, and what happens when that support is lacking?

8 What kind of social and emotional education might help classmates understand and interact more positively with students who have special needs?

9 Make a discussion question based on the information you have obtained for "Ask AI."

Debate

1 Inclusive education should be prioritized over specialized schools for students with special needs. (Focus: inclusive education vs. special schools)

Agree	Disagree

2 Schools should prioritize educational equity for diverse learners over academic excellence and standardized performance. (Focus: educational equity vs. academic excellence)

Agree	Disagree

3 Training all general education teachers in special education is more effective than hiring additional special education specialists. (Focus: teacher training vs. specialist hiring)

Agree	Disagree

4 The rights of students with disabilities should outweigh community objections when building special schools. (Focus: disability rights vs. community concerns)

Agree	Disagree

ⓘ Wrap-Up: Your Turn to Write

Prompt: *Reflect on what inclusive education means to you. Should students with special needs be taught in regular classrooms? Explain your opinion with reasons and examples.*

Sample Essay

Inclusive education means more than placing students with special needs in regular classrooms; it means giving them the support they need to succeed. I believe students with special needs should be included in regular schools whenever possible, but only when the proper support systems are in place.

Learning together can benefit all students. When children with and without disabilities share a classroom, they can learn empathy, patience, and respect. I remember a classmate with ADHD in elementary school. At first, we were confused by his behavior, but with help from our teacher, we learned how to include him and work together as a team. It made us more cooperative and understanding.

However, inclusion should not be forced. If schools do not provide trained teachers, aides, or assistive tools, students with special needs may feel frustrated or left behind. In some cases, separate special education classes or schools may be better, especially for students with severe intellectual disabilities or emotional challenges. These students may need more personalized support than a regular classroom can provide.

Even when students are in special programs, they should still have chances to interact with others through school events or shared activities. This helps reduce stigma and build community. Some people think students with disabilities slow down the class, but this is a misunderstanding. Every student learns differently. Our education system should recognize and respect those differences.

In conclusion, I support inclusive education, but only if schools are truly ready. With trained teachers, proper resources, and an accepting environment, inclusive classrooms can be positive spaces where all students grow together.

💡 My Reflections and Notes

Write down key insights, teaching ideas, personal reflections, or any information you want to remember.

Chapter 09

Beyond the Test —
Rethinking Education Through the International Baccalaureate Lens

Warm-Up

- Have you ever heard of the International Baccalaureate (IB) program? What do you know about it?
- How is IB education different from the traditional Korean education system?
- Do you think Korean students would benefit from a curriculum that includes essays, discussions, and independent research?
- If you had the choice, would you prefer to study in an IB school or a regular Korean high school? Why?

Introduction

In recent years, the International Baccalaureate (IB) has drawn increasing attention in Korea as a progressive alternative to the traditional education system. Originally designed in Switzerland for the children of globally mobile families, the IB program now operates in over 150 countries and is recognized by universities around the world. Its reputation for encouraging critical thinking, intercultural understanding, and holistic development has prompted a growing number of Korean educators and policymakers to explore its potential in local schools.

The core of the IB philosophy is fundamentally different from Korea's exam-driven approach. While Korean schools tend to emphasize memorization, multiple-choice testing, and lecture-based instruction, especially in preparation for the CSAT (College Scholastic Ability Test), IB promotes inquiry-based learning, interdisciplinary understanding, and student-led exploration. Students engage in collaborative projects, write extended essays, reflect on their learning, and participate in discussions that require them to evaluate global and ethical issues. Success in the IB is not determined solely by test scores but by a student's ability to think independently and apply knowledge creatively.

In response to this growing interest, Korea has begun experimenting with "Korean IB" (KIB), a version of the IB curriculum delivered in Korean. Pilot programs have launched in a few public schools across the country, raising both hopes and concerns. Supporters see it as a chance to reduce the overwhelming pressure of private education and nurture more self-directed, globally competent learners. Critics, however, point to the challenges of aligning IB assessment methods with the Korean university entrance system and question whether the national culture of education is ready to embrace such radical change.

This chapter explores the principles of the IB, how it is being adapted to Korean schools, and what lessons it holds for the future of Korean education. Can IB be a realistic model for reform, or is it just another educational experiment?

👤 Chitchat with Mates

1 Have you ever studied in a classroom where you were asked to lead discussions or do independent research? Describe your experience.

	Answers
Me	
Mate 1	
Mate 2	
Mate 3	

2 Do you think Korean students would enjoy writing long essays and doing presentations instead of taking written tests? Why or why not?

	Answers
Me	
Mate 1	
Mate 2	
Mate 3	

3 How do you think parents in Korea would react to a school that doesn't focus on grades or rankings?

	Answers
Me	
Mate 1	
Mate 2	
Mate 3	

4 Would you like to attend a school where you can choose topics to study based on your interests? Why or why not?

	Answers
Me	
Mate 1	
Mate 2	
Mate 3	

 In-depth Reading

Reimagining Learning: The Promise and Challenge of IB in Korea

In Korea's highly competitive education landscape, the introduction of the International Baccalaureate (IB) marks a significant shift in both philosophy and practice. Originally developed in the 1960s by educators in Geneva, Switzerland, the IB was designed to offer a consistent, internationally accepted curriculum for students who moved frequently across borders. Over the decades, however, it has grown into a prestigious academic program adopted by over 5,000 schools worldwide, offering four main programs: the Primary Years Programme (PYP), Middle Years Programme (MYP), Diploma Programme (DP), and Career-related Programme (CP).

The most well-known is the IB Diploma Programme (IBDP), a rigorous two-year course of study for students aged 16–19. Students take six subjects across different disciplines and complete three core components: the Extended Essay (EE), a 4,000-word independent research paper; the Theory of Knowledge (TOK), a course that explores how we know what we know; and Creativity, Activity, Service (CAS), which encourages students to engage in extracurricular and community projects. These components are designed not only to build academic strength but also to develop global-mindedness, ethical reasoning, and real-world problem-solving.

IB's holistic approach contrasts sharply with Korea's test-centered system and offers a model that values thinking over memorization, exploration over repetition, and depth over coverage. It is this fundamental reimagining of what it means to learn, and why we learn, that makes IB both a bold opportunity and a complex challenge for Korea's education system.

Why IB Appeals to Korean Educators and Policymakers

IB's rising popularity in Korea is part of a broader desire to reform the national education system. For decades, Korean schools have been shaped by CSAT preparation, heavy reliance on rote learning, and high private education costs. Critics argue that this system narrows students' creativity, limits their emotional development, and places too much pressure on standardized testing.

In contrast, IB emphasizes depth over breadth, process over product, and inquiry over answers. It aligns with 21st-century education goals, such as global competence, critical thinking, and interdisciplinary learning. For policymakers, the IB presents a model of future-ready education. For teachers, it offers a more flexible curriculum. And for students, it creates opportunities for self-expression, global engagement, and academic independence.

To adapt IB to the local context, the Ministry of Education and the Jeju Provincial Office of Education launched a Korean-language version of IB (KIB) starting with pilot programs in Jeju. KIB retains the core framework of IB but delivers content in Korean, allowing local students to benefit from IB's educational approach without facing an additional language barrier.

The introduction of KIB aims to reduce educational inequality by making elite international curricula accessible to public school students. It also responds to rising concerns about private school dominance and the lack of creativity in public education. However, the initiative is still in its early stages, and many logistical and philosophical questions remain unresolved.

Challenges in the Korean Context

Implementing IB in Korea is far from straightforward. First, the Korean college admission system is deeply rooted in GPA, class rankings, and CSAT scores. While some Korean universities have started recognizing IB diplomas, most still rely on traditional metrics for admission. This creates a mismatch: students in IB programs may gain valuable skills but find themselves disadvantaged when applying to Korean universities.

Second, teachers must undergo extensive training to deliver the IB curriculum. This includes learning how to design inquiry-based lessons, assess open-ended tasks, and support students through independent projects. Many Korean teachers are used to textbook-driven, exam-focused instruction and may struggle with the pedagogical shift. Teacher burnout, lack of resources, and unclear institutional support also pose major hurdles.

Third, parents' expectations can be a barrier. Many parents are unfamiliar with IB's philosophy and may view its alternative assessment methods, such as rubrics, reflections, and portfolios, as unreliable compared to standardized tests. They may worry that a non-traditional education could harm their child's competitiveness in college admissions.

IB in the Korean Classroom

Despite these challenges, IB offers notable advantages. It encourages students to take ownership of their learning, develop time management and research skills, and explore interdisciplinary connections. In a culture where academic success is often defined by conformity and repetition, IB nurtures curiosity, individuality, and intrinsic motivation.

IB also fosters a global perspective. Through TOK, students engage with philosophical questions and different cultural worldviews. Through CAS, they serve their communities and reflect on personal growth. These experiences help students become not just good test takers, but thoughtful, empathetic, and active members of society.

Additionally, IB assessment methods prioritize reasoning, synthesis, and application. Students are not rewarded simply for memorizing facts but for demonstrating understanding through essays, presentations, and oral exams. This shift in evaluation encourages deeper learning and better prepares students for university-level study.

In Jeju and several private international schools that offer the IBDP, early feedback is mixed but promising. Students report that while IB is demanding, it is also more meaningful. One student remarked, "I feel like I'm learning how to think, not just how to solve test questions." Teachers, after initial adjustment, say they enjoy more freedom to design lessons and interact with students in more dynamic ways.

However, schools also report that workload management is a serious issue. Some students feel overwhelmed by the number of essays and deadlines. Others say that transitioning from CSAT-style instruction to open-ended learning was difficult at first. Support systems such as academic advising and mental health services are key to student success in IB environments.

The Future of IB in Korea

Whether IB can be successfully integrated into the Korean education system remains an open question. If college admissions policies begin to reward IB-style learning outcomes such as critical thinking, writing ability, and project-based work, then IB could drive meaningful change. However, if the current test-centered model persists, IB may remain a niche option for only a few students.

What's clear is that the IB debate touches on deeper questions: What should education be for? What kinds of citizens do we want to raise? And how can we balance academic rigor with emotional well-being and creativity? For future teachers, understanding IB's philosophy, even if not directly involved in the program, is a valuable professional asset. It broadens one's vision of what teaching can look like and opens the door to alternative approaches that prioritize learning as a process, not just a performance.

🔍 Comprehension Questions

1 What are the core features of the IB Diploma Programme, and how do they differ from traditional Korean education?

2 What is Korean IB, and why was it introduced?

3 What are the challenges that schools and teachers face when implementing IB in Korea?

4 How does the IB approach benefit students in ways that standardized test-focused education does not?

5 According to the essay, what needs to change in Korea for IB to have a wider impact?

 **Ask AI**

What are the key aspects of IB education in Japan?

In-depth Discussion Questions

1 How might student behavior and classroom dynamics change if Korean schools replaced lecture-style teaching with the IB's inquiry-based learning model focused on exploration and discussion?

2 What kinds of professional development and classroom resources would Korean teachers need to successfully adopt the IB approach in public schools?

3 Should Korean universities revise their admissions criteria to better accommodate IB-style assessments like essays, projects, and portfolios? Why or why not?

4 How could wider adoption of IB or KIB programs reduce Korea's dependence on private education and the *hagwon* system?

5 What emotional or psychological changes might students experience when shifting from a test-centered system to IB's more open-ended, student-driven learning style?

6 Do you think IB programs should be introduced in more public schools across Korea, or should they remain optional and limited to certain regions or schools? Explain your answer.

7 How can schools help Korean parents understand and accept the value of IB education when it lacks traditional grades and rankings?

8 If you could design a hybrid system combining the structure of Korean education and the creativity of IB, what would it include and why?

9 Make a discussion question based on the information you have obtained for "Ask AI."

💬 Debate

1 Korean public schools should fully adopt the IB curriculum instead of continuing with the traditional CSAT-focused system. (Focus: innovation vs. national standards)

Agree	Disagree

2 The IB program is better suited for international contexts and should not be applied broadly in Korea's public education. (Focus: global adaptability vs. local relevance)

Agree	Disagree

3 IB's essay- and project-based assessments provide a more accurate measure of student ability than Korea's standardized exams. (Focus: holistic assessment vs. objective testing)

Agree	Disagree

4 Parents should be free to choose IB or traditional education paths without government interference or pressure. (Focus: educational freedom vs. national policy)

Agree	Disagree

🧭 Wrap-Up: Your Turn to Write

Prompt: *Do you believe the International Baccalaureate can realistically improve Korean education? Explain your opinion and approach as a future teacher working in Korean schools.*

Sample Essay

I believe the International Baccalaureate (IB) offers valuable lessons for Korea's education system, but full adoption may not be realistic yet. As a future teacher, I support incorporating elements of IB, such as inquiry-based learning, interdisciplinary projects, and reflective assessments, into Korean classrooms, especially as we move toward future-ready education. However, I also recognize the unique pressures and expectations that shape Korean schools.

One key strength of IB is its focus on thinking, not just memorizing. Korean students are intelligent and hardworking, but too often, education becomes a race to master test formats. IB's approach encourages students to ask questions, connect subjects, and take initiative. These skills are essential in today's global society. Programs like Theory of Knowledge and Extended Essay help students become independent thinkers—something our test-driven system rarely promotes.

However, there are also barriers. Korea's college admissions system still depends heavily on CSAT scores and GPAs. Unless universities start recognizing IB assessments more widely, students in IB programs may face disadvantages when applying to Korean schools. Teachers also need significant retraining, and many parents are skeptical of unfamiliar methods that don't include rankings.

In conclusion, I believe Korea should not copy IB entirely but learn from it. Schools can adopt project-based tasks, student reflection, and global themes without abandoning our national curriculum. As a teacher, I hope to blend the strengths of both systems and create classrooms where curiosity matters as much as correctness.

💡 My Reflections and Notes

Write down key insights, teaching ideas, personal reflections, or any information you want to remember.

Extra: More About IB

Understanding the IB Curriculum

The International Baccalaureate (IB) is a global education program designed to help students think critically, learn independently, and become responsible global citizens. It focuses not just on what students learn, but how they learn, and why that learning matters in real life. The IB is made up of four programs, depending on a student's age.

1. **Primary Years Programme (PYP): Ages 3-12 (Kindergarten to Grade 5)**
   - Encourages children to ask questions and explore topics through hands-on learning.
   - Subjects like language, math, science, and art are taught through big themes like "Who We Are" or "How the World Works."
   - Students complete a final group project called the PYP Exhibition, where they research a real-world issue and present solutions.

2. **Middle Years Programme (MYP): Ages 11-16 (Grades 6 to 10)**
   - Focuses on connecting school subjects to everyday life and real-world problems.
   - Students take eight subjects, including design (technology), languages, and physical education.
   - In the final year, students complete a Personal Project, choosing a topic they care about and creating something original like a book, a video, or an invention.

3. **Diploma Programme (DP): Ages 16-19 (Grades 11–12)**
   - This is the most well-known IB program. Students study six subjects (math, languages, science, etc.) and also complete three key components:
     - Extended Essay (EE): A research paper on a topic the student chooses.
     - Theory of Knowledge (TOK): A class about how we know what we

know.
- Creativity, Activity, Service (CAS): Volunteer work, arts, or physical activity that helps develop the whole person.
• Students are assessed through essays, projects, and exams, not just multiple-choice tests.

4. **Career-related Programme (CP): Ages 16-19**
   • Combines IB academic courses with career-related studies like business, IT, or healthcare.
   • Great for students who want a balance of practical skills and academic learning.

What Makes IB Different?

• Global Perspective: Students learn to think about issues from international and ethical viewpoints.
• Focus on Skills: IB helps students become critical thinkers, strong communicators, and lifelong learners.
• Less Memorization: IB values essays, presentations, and research more than just test-taking.

Teaching the IB Way

If you're a teacher or future teacher working in a Korean school adopting the International Baccalaureate (IB) or Korean IB (KIB), your role shifts significantly. Instead of focusing on delivering content for exams, your goal becomes guiding inquiry, supporting reflection, and encouraging global thinking. Here's a breakdown of how to teach effectively in an IB-style classroom:

1. Shift from Lecturer to Facilitator
• Traditional role: Deliver content, explain concepts, assign practice
• IB role: Ask open-ended questions, support students in exploring

answers themselves
- Example: Instead of teaching a history timeline, ask: "How might history look different if told from another country's point of view?"

2. Design Inquiry-Based Lessons

- Lessons start with a question or problem, not a worksheet.
- Encourage students to investigate, experiment, and reflect.
- Use real-world issues or case studies.

Example structure

- Provocation: Present a surprising image or quote.
- Inquiry: Students ask questions.
- Research: Students work in groups using various sources.
- Reflection: Share and compare findings.

3. Emphasize Skills over Memorization

- Teach research, critical thinking, communication, and reflection.
- Use projects, presentations, and portfolios.
- Allow students to choose how to demonstrate understanding.

4. Encourage Student Voice and Choice

- Let students pick essay topics, reading texts, or project formats.
- In CAS (or similar KIB elements), guide students in selecting meaningful service or creative activities.

5. Assess with Rubrics, Not Just Tests

- Use clear rubrics that evaluate thinking, reasoning, creativity, and expression.
- Give ongoing feedback to help students revise and improve.
- Include self-assessment and peer feedback.

6. Integrate Global and Ethical Perspectives

- Link lessons to global contexts: identity, culture, sustainability, innovation.
- Ask students to consider ethical questions: "What is a fair solution?" "Who benefits or loses?"

7. Teach Reflection
- Have students keep journals or reflection logs.
- After a project or discussion, ask: "What did you learn about yourself?" "What would you do differently next time?"

8. Collaborate Across Subjects
- Plan units with colleagues that connect subjects—e.g., a science and geography project on water pollution.
- Highlight interdisciplinary learning (a key feature in MYP and DP).

9. Build Relationships and Emotional Support
- IB values student well-being. Show interest in students' passions and goals.
- Encourage a safe classroom where questions and mistakes are welcome.

10. Use English, But Support Korean When Needed (KIB)
- In KIB, lessons may be in Korean but still follow IB's methods.
- Use bilingual strategies, especially for difficult concepts, while promoting English communication when possible.

Teaching in the IB model isn't about being an "answer giver." It's about helping students think deeply, take ownership of their learning, and become confident, ethical learners.

Chapter 10

Talking About What Matters — Rethinking Sex Education in a Changing World

Warm-Up

- When did you first learn about sex education, and what do you remember about it?

- Do you think sex education should start in elementary school? Why or why not?

- How do social media and the internet affect teenagers' understanding of sex and relationships?

- Should sex education focus more on abstinence or on safe and responsible choices?

Introduction

Sex education has long been one of the most sensitive and controversial topics in school curricula, especially in conservative societies like South Korea. While puberty, reproduction, and relationships are universal parts of human life, how and when we talk about them remains hotly debated. In today's fast-changing world, students are often exposed to sexual content through social media, YouTube, online pornography, and TV far earlier than formal education can address. As a result, schools are under growing pressure to provide timely, accurate, and responsible sex education.

Currently, the official sex education curriculum in Korea varies by age group. Elementary schools introduce basic ideas about body changes and safety. Middle schools cover reproduction and gender roles. High schools may go further into contraception, sexually transmitted diseases (STDs), and sexual responsibility. However, critics say the curriculum is outdated, vague, and avoids essential issues like LGBTQ+ identities, consent, and digital safety.

There is also a cultural tension between abstinence-focused education and more open discussions of birth control and safe sex. Traditional values discourage premarital sex and emphasize the role of the family in teaching morals. But in reality, many parents feel uncomfortable or unprepared to talk about these topics, leaving schools and increasingly the internet as the main sources of information for teens.

Teachers often struggle with how much to say and how to say it. Some fear backlash from parents or school administrators. Others lack the training or confidence to deal with complex, sensitive questions. Meanwhile, students are left to navigate a flood of online content—some educational, much of it misleading or harmful.

This chapter explores the current state and future direction of sex education in Korea, asking how schools, families, and society can work together to protect and prepare young people for the realities of life and relationships.

👤 Chitchat with Mates

1 Did your schools—elementary, middle, and high school—provide sex education? What was it like?

	Answers
Me	
Mate 1	
Mate 2	
Mate 3	

2 Who do you think should teach students about sex—parents, teachers, or mature friends? Why?

	Answers
Me	
Mate 1	
Mate 2	
Mate 3	

3 Do you think students talk about sex more openly online or in person? Explain your answer.

	Answers
Me	
Mate 1	
Mate 2	
Mate 3	

4 How does social media influence what young people think about love and relationships?

	Answers
Me	
Mate 1	
Mate 2	
Mate 3	

 In-depth Reading

Current Structure of Sex Education

Sex education is not just about biology; it's about life, safety, responsibility, and identity. In a rapidly digitalizing and diversifying society like South Korea, the need for comprehensive and relevant sex education has never been greater. Yet many schools, teachers, and families continue to struggle with how to teach it effectively, appropriately, and openly. The gap between what students need to know and what schools are willing, or allowed, to teach is widening, especially in a world filled with online content that is often misleading or harmful.

In South Korea, sex education is included in school curriculums from elementary to high school, but its content is often limited. In elementary schools, students learn about physical growth and personal hygiene. Middle school programs may cover reproductive health and basic information about puberty. High school curriculums may include contraception, sexually transmitted diseases (STDs), and family planning. However, the material is usually taught through short lessons in health classes or integrated into science or ethics subjects, often without depth or student engagement.

Teachers are expected to follow government guidelines, which emphasize abstinence and traditional family values. As a result, topics such as sexual orientation, gender identity, emotional relationships, consent, and digital safety are often omitted or only briefly mentioned. Many students report that sex education classes feel awkward, overly simplistic, or moralistic, rather than informative or empowering.

The Influence of Media and Online Platforms

While formal education may avoid controversial topics, students are learning about sex from other sources, mainly the internet. YouTube, online forums, social media platforms, and even pornography often become their informal teachers. Some of this content is educational and positive, but much of it promotes distorted views of relationships, gender roles, and sexual behavior.

Exposure to explicit content through smartphones and social media is now a daily reality for many teens. Without proper guidance, students may develop unhealthy attitudes toward consent, body image, intimacy, and gender expectations. Some may even be vulnerable to grooming, online harassment, or sharing private images without understanding the consequences. In this context, schools cannot afford to stay silent or neutral. They must prepare students for digital life as much as for physical life.

Controversial Topics: LGBTQ+, Birth Control, and Abstinence

One of the biggest challenges in updating sex education in Korea is the cultural discomfort surrounding topics such as premarital sex, homosexuality, and birth control. Conservative values remain strong, and many parents and educators worry that discussing these issues will encourage early sexual behavior. This fear has led to an emphasis on abstinence-only education, which discourages sex before marriage but often fails to provide information about contraception or safe practices for those who do become sexually active.

LGBTQ+ issues are particularly sensitive. Although awareness and advocacy have grown among youth, LGBTQ+ topics are still rarely included in official curriculums. Many teachers feel unprepared to talk about gender identity or same-sex relationships, and those who try may face backlash from parents or school authorities. As a result, students who identify as LGBTQ+ often feel invisible, isolated, or ashamed in classrooms that do not recognize their experiences.

Comprehensive sex education does not promote early sexual activity; it equips students with the knowledge to make responsible decisions. When students understand how their bodies work, how to protect themselves, and how to build healthy relationships, they are more likely to delay sexual activity and avoid risky behavior. Teaching about consent, boundaries, respect, and inclusivity helps all students, regardless of their background or orientation.

Importantly, topics such as sexual violence and dating violence must be addressed clearly. Students need to know how to recognize abusive behaviors, set boundaries, seek help, and protect themselves in both online and offline relationships.

The Role of Teachers and Parents

Teachers play a key role in delivering sex education, but many are not adequately trained. Some feel uncomfortable discussing sensitive topics in front of students or worry about how parents will respond. Others simply do not know how to approach complex issues like sexual harassment, gender identity, or digital safety in age-appropriate ways.

Training and professional development are essential. Teachers need clear guidelines, access to up-to-date resources, and a safe environment where they can teach without fear of controversy. Schools must also foster open communication with parents so that families understand the purpose and content of sex education programs. In fact, the role of parents should not be underestimated. When families talk openly about sex, relationships, and values at home, students are more likely to have healthy attitudes and behaviors. Unfortunately, many Korean parents still avoid these conversations due to discomfort, lack of knowledge, or traditional beliefs.

Sex education should be a shared responsibility between home and school. Parents can provide values and context, while schools offer accurate information and professional guidance.

Looking Ahead: A New Model for a New Generation

The world has changed, and sex education must change with it. Young people today are growing up in a digital landscape filled with both opportunities and dangers. They are exposed to images, messages, and expectations about sex and relationships from a very early age. If we do not educate them, someone, or something, else will.

A modern sex education curriculum should start early, be age-appropriate, and evolve with students as they mature. It should cover physical, emotional, and digital aspects of relationships. Key topics should include anatomy, consent, gender identity, contraception, STDs, online safety, healthy communication, and respect for diversity. Programs should reflect the real questions and situations that young people face today.

The Netherlands, for example, is often cited as a model for effective sex education. Starting as early as age four, Dutch students learn about respect, boundaries, and relationships in age-appropriate ways. By the time they reach adolescence, they receive clear, science-based information about contraception, STDs, and consent. This early and open approach has led to lower rates of teen pregnancy and sexually transmitted infections compared to other countries. Dutch sex education emphasizes not just physical health, but emotional well-being and mutual respect, demonstrating that open, honest education can lead to more informed and responsible young people.

Schools need national support, clear policies, and proper funding. Teachers must be trained, trusted, and protected from unnecessary political pressure. And families must be part of the conversation, breaking the silence that has made sex a taboo topic for too long.

Most importantly, students must be treated not as passive receivers of rules, but as individuals with the right to accurate information, respect, and guidance. Sex education is not just about preventing problems; it's about preparing students for real life, real relationships, and responsible choices.

Comprehension Questions

1 What are some of the main limitations of sex education currently provided in South Korean schools?

2 How does exposure to online content and social media influence students' understanding of sex and relationships?

3 Why is it important to include topics like sexual violence and dating violence in modern sex education curriculums?

4 What challenges do Korean teachers face when trying to deliver effective sex education?

5 How does the Netherlands approach sex education, and what are some of its outcomes?

 **Ask AI**

What are crucial components in secondary school sex education in the United Kingdom?

❓ In-depth Discussion Questions

1 Why do you think sex education remains a taboo subject in many Korean schools and homes, even though students are already exposed to sexual content through media and the internet?

_____
_____
_____
_____
_____

2 What are the potential dangers of students learning about sex mainly through pornography or social media instead of formal education provided by schools and trained teachers?

_____
_____
_____
_____
_____

3 How might including LGBTQ+ issues in sex education help build a more inclusive environment, and what challenges might arise in doing so in a conservative cultural context?

_____
_____
_____
_____
_____

4 What kind of training and support should teachers receive to confidently teach topics such as consent, gender identity, and online sexual safety in the classroom?

_____
_____
_____
_____
_____
_____

5 How can parents and schools work together to provide consistent and effective sex education, especially when values and levels of comfort about these topics may differ?

_____
_____
_____
_____
_____
_____

6 In what ways can school-based education help students recognize early signs of sexual violence or dating abuse, and how can schools provide appropriate support systems?

_____
_____
_____
_____
_____
_____

7 Why is it important to start sex education from a young age and gradually increase its depth as students grow older and face new physical and emotional challenges?

8 What can South Korea learn from the Netherlands' approach to sex education, and how can those ideas be adapted to fit Korean cultural values and school systems?

9 Make a discussion question based on the information you have obtained for "Ask AI."

🗨 Debate

1 Comprehensive sex education should replace abstinence-based programs in schools. (Focus: comprehensive education vs. abstinence-only education)

Agree	Disagree

2 Schools should take greater responsibility than parents in delivering sex education. (Focus: school responsibility vs. parental authority)

Agree	Disagree

3 Sex education should include LGBTQ+ topics to promote inclusivity and respect for diversity. (Focus: inclusive curriculum vs. traditional values)

Agree	Disagree

4 Media literacy is a better solution than internet censorship to protect students from harmful sexual content. (Focus: media literacy vs. online restriction)

Agree	Disagree

ⓘ Wrap-Up: Your Turn to Write

Prompt: *Do you think current sex education in Korean schools is enough? What changes should be made? Share your opinion and explain your reasons with examples.*

Sample Essay

I believe that sex education in Korean schools is not enough for today's students. Although it is included in the curriculum, the lessons are often brief, awkward, and focus only on biological facts. Many important topics, such as consent, emotional relationships, LGBTQ+ issues, and digital safety, are not properly discussed.

For example, students often hear about contraception and STDs only in high school, when many are already exposed to sexual content through the internet. Without proper guidance, some may believe false information from social media or online pornography. This can lead to dangerous misunderstandings about relationships and sexual behavior.

I also think schools should teach students about sexual violence and dating abuse. Many teenagers are starting relationships, but they don't always know what is healthy or harmful. If students learn about boundaries, respect, and how to ask for help, they will be better prepared to protect themselves and others.

Teachers should be given more training and support so they can teach these topics with confidence. At the same time, parents should be more involved in talking with their children at home. Sex education should not be a one-time lesson, but an ongoing conversation.

We can also learn from other countries like the Netherlands, where sex education starts early and focuses on respect, feelings, and safety. Their open and honest approach has led to better outcomes for students.

In conclusion, Korean sex education needs to change. Students deserve more honest, inclusive, and practical lessons that prepare them for the realities of growing up. We cannot protect young people by staying silent; we must give them the knowledge to make safe and respectful choices.

💡 My Reflections and Notes

Write down key insights, teaching ideas, personal reflections, or any information you want to remember.

Chapter 11

College Life Unfiltered — From Club Fairs to Career Fears

Warm-Up

- What were your expectations before entering college, and have they matched your actual experience?
- Do you think your current major suits your interests and strengths?
- What worries you most about your future after graduation?
- Have you participated in any clubs, internships, or exchange programs during college?

Introduction

College is often described as a time of freedom, exploration, and self-discovery. After the intense academic pressure of high school and the long-awaited college entrance process, many Korean students expect university life to offer relaxation, personal growth, and exciting new opportunities. However, once on campus, students quickly realize that college is not just about enjoying freedom; it's also a time of uncertainty, complex decisions, and invisible pressures that shape their future paths.

One of the most common struggles students face is a mismatch between their major and personal interests. Many students choose their department based on entrance scores, job prospects, or family advice rather than genuine passion. As a result, they may feel lost, unmotivated, or even trapped in a field that doesn't align with who they are. Changing majors is possible, but not always easy or socially encouraged, especially in competitive academic environments.

At the same time, the pressure to prepare for a successful career begins almost immediately. Students are expected to gain more than just academic knowledge; they must also build resumes filled with internships, certifications, club activities, volunteer experience, and language proficiency. This can create a competitive atmosphere where students feel constantly behind, even while attending classes and participating in campus life. Many students report feeling anxious or confused about what path to take after graduation.

In addition, college offers chances for study abroad, exchange programs, and participation in student clubs and leadership activities. These experiences can be rewarding and eye-opening, but they are not equally accessible to all. Financial limitations, grade requirements, and lack of information can prevent many students from taking full advantage of these programs.

This chapter explores the multifaceted nature of Korean college life—its possibilities and its pressures. From mismatched majors to unclear futures, we examine how students navigate their years on campus, and what "success" really means in this unique stage of life. How can students make the most of their college experience, even when the path ahead feels uncertain?

👤 Chitchat with Mates

1 What surprised you the most about college life compared to what you expected in high school?

	Answers
Me	
Mate 1	
Mate 2	
Mate 3	

2 Have you ever thought about changing your major? If so, why or why not? And if you have, what major do you wish to pursue?

	Answers
Me	
Mate 1	
Mate 2	
Mate 3	

3 What kind of job or career are you considering after graduation? Why do you wish to have that job?

	Answers
Me	
Mate 1	
Mate 2	
Mate 3	

4 Have you joined any clubs, circles, or programs that made your college life more meaningful?

	Answers
Me	
Mate 1	
Mate 2	
Mate 3	

 In-depth Reading

Expectations vs. Reality

College life is often imagined as a time of freedom, discovery, and self-development. After surviving Korea's intense high school system and the high-stakes CSAT, many students look forward to university as a well-earned break and a chance to pursue their interests. For years, students anticipate this next chapter as a time to make their own decisions, meet new friends, explore diverse experiences, and gain independence from rigid academic structures. Popular media, older siblings, and social expectations further contribute to the idea that college is a golden period of personal growth and memorable adventures.

However, the reality of college life is often more complicated than the idealized version seen in media or imagined during high school. Freedom does exist, but it often comes packaged with confusion, pressure, and new responsibilities that many students feel unprepared to manage. With less structured schedules, students must learn how to manage their own time, make decisions about their academic paths, and begin thinking seriously about their careers. For many, this transition can feel overwhelming, especially when they realize that college demands as much, if not more, focus and self-discipline than high school.

Mismatch Between Major and Passion

One of the most common issues Korean college students face is a mismatch between their major and their interests or aptitudes. Because many students choose their major based on university rankings, job market trends, or parental expectations, they often enter college without a clear sense of personal direction. Some discover early on that they dislike their field of study, while others gradually feel disconnected as their classes fail to spark genuine interest or motivation.

Changing majors is an option, but bureaucratic hurdles, peer pressure, financial considerations, and fear of falling behind can discourage students from making the switch. There's also a social stigma in Korea surrounding indecision or perceived instability, which adds another emotional barrier to such changes. This disconnect often leads to disengagement in class, poor academic performance, and increasing anxiety about the future. Some students endure their major without passion simply to graduate, while others silently struggle with the fear that they have made an irreversible mistake.

Career Preparation and the Resume Race

Another major concern is career preparation. In today's competitive job market, students are expected not only to perform academically, but also to build diverse portfolios. Internships, certifications, language scores, part-time jobs, and club activities are no longer optional; they are considered essential. The phrase "spec-building" has become a central part of student life, referring to the accumulation of qualifications and experiences that may appeal to future employers.

This constant pressure can be overwhelming, especially when students do not have clear guidance or when they compare themselves to others who seem more prepared. Social media platforms like Instagram and LinkedIn add to this pressure, as students are constantly exposed to peers' achievements, internships, and overseas programs. Many feel like they're running a race without knowing where the finish line is, trying to check every box without time to reflect on whether it suits them personally.

In this race, the meaning of education can sometimes become blurred. Learning may take a backseat to credentialing. Students may feel pressured to participate in activities not because they're interested, but because they are told they "should." This mindset can lead to burnout, especially by the third or fourth year, when students are expected to juggle graduation requirements, job applications, and possibly even postgraduate plans.

Study Abroad, Campus Life, and Social Pressure

In the midst of these pressures, students also try to enjoy the unique opportunities that college offers. Study abroad programs, exchange semesters, and language training courses are highly sought after for those who can afford them. These experiences help broaden perspectives, improve English communication skills, and build confidence. They are often described as "once-in-a-lifetime" chances to experience a new culture and expand one's worldview.

However, such programs are often competitive and expensive, limiting access for many students. Application requirements, such as GPA cutoffs or high English proficiency test scores, can discourage participation. Financial limitations also prevent many students from even considering international programs. This further widens the gap between those with strong financial or informational support and those without, reinforcing inequality even at the university level.

Student clubs and campus life also play an important role in shaping the college experience. Whether joining a major-related society, a volunteer group, or a hobby circle, students often find community, identity, and support through peer interaction. These groups can be sources of creativity, stress relief, and leadership experience. For many students, clubs offer the emotional connection that helps them endure academic or career stress.

However, not all students benefit equally. Some may find it hard to connect due to shyness, academic workload, or lack of inclusive environments. Clubs that operate through alumni networks or social drinking may feel intimidating or exclusive. First-generation college students, or those juggling part-time jobs and family responsibilities, may feel left out of social life on campus. Balancing social life with academic and career pressure remains a challenge for many, and some end up feeling isolated even in a busy campus.

Uncertainty About the Future

Adding to these external challenges is an often unspoken internal one: uncertainty about the future. Even students with strong academic records and active resumes may feel lost when asked, "What do you want to do after graduation?" In a fast-changing economy with unstable job prospects, the path to adulthood feels increasingly unpredictable. The rise of AI, automation, and global competition adds new layers of complexity to career planning.

Many students express concern about employability, career fit, and long-term satisfaction. These concerns are not just practical but deeply emotional, affecting students' confidence and mental health. The fear of making the "wrong" choice often leads to hesitation and anxiety. In some cases, students avoid making any decision at all, delaying graduation or pursuing graduate school simply to postpone facing the job market.

In response to these realities, universities are beginning to offer more career counseling, mentorship programs, and interdisciplinary opportunities. Some schools now provide more flexible curricula and encourage cross-major exploration. However, much of the burden still falls on students to navigate their own way. Some succeed in building meaningful experiences and career pathways; others struggle quietly, uncertain about whether they are doing college "right." The pressure to excel often overshadows the importance of exploration and self-reflection.

🔍 Comprehension Questions

1 Why do many Korean students experience a mismatch between their major and their personal interests or abilities after entering college?

_____
_____

2 What kinds of activities are students expected to complete in order to build a competitive resume during college?

_____
_____

3 What are some challenges that limit access to study abroad or exchange programs for many students?

_____
_____

4 How do student clubs and campus life contribute to a student's college experience, and what difficulties do some students face in participating?

_____
_____

5 According to the essay, what emotional impact does uncertainty about the future have on college students?

_____
_____

 **Ask AI**

What are popular student activities at the University of Melbourne?

In-depth Discussion Questions

1 Why do you think so many students realize their major doesn't suit them after entering college? What can be done to help students make more informed decisions before choosing their field of study?

2 How does the pressure to build a competitive resume during college affect students' mental health and sense of identity? Should universities redefine what it means to be "career ready"?

3 Do you think study abroad and exchange programs should be more accessible to all students? What policies or campus initiatives could reduce financial and academic barriers?

4 How do social expectations about job prestige influence students' decisions in college? Are students choosing paths for themselves, or for others?

_____
_____
_____
_____
_____
_____
_____

5 In what ways can student clubs and campus organizations support those who feel disconnected or overwhelmed? What makes a student group truly inclusive?

_____
_____
_____
_____
_____
_____
_____

6 Should universities do more to support students who want to change majors or explore interdisciplinary paths? What kind of system would reduce the fear of falling behind?

_____
_____
_____
_____
_____
_____
_____

7 What advice would you give to a freshman who feels uncertain about their future? How can older students or professors play a more active role in mentoring?

8 How can we balance the idea that college should be both a time for personal growth and a preparation stage for employment? Are these goals in conflict or can they be combined meaningfully?

9 Make a discussion question based on the information you have obtained for "Ask AI."

💬 Debate

1 Universities should allow students to change majors freely without restrictions or penalties. (Focus: student exploration vs. academic structure)

Agree	Disagree

2 Career preparation is more important than academic learning in college. (Focus: employability vs. intellectual development)

Agree	Disagree

3 Study abroad and exchange programs should be fully funded by universities for all students. (Focus: equal opportunity vs. financial practicality)

Agree	Disagree

4 Student clubs are essential for college success and should be mandatory for first-year students. (Focus: community building vs. personal freedom)

Agree	Disagree

ⓘ Wrap-Up: Your Turn to Write

Prompt: *What do you think is the biggest challenge college students face today—academic pressure, career preparation, or uncertainty about the future? Reflect on your own experience or observations, and suggest how students or schools can respond to this challenge.*

> **Sample Essay**

In my opinion, the biggest challenge college students face today is uncertainty about the future. While academic stress and career preparation are also serious concerns, uncertainty affects everything from how students choose classes to how they manage their time, motivation, and mental health.

Many students enter college with high hopes but no clear direction. They may choose a major based on university rankings, job trends, or parental influence, only to realize later that they are not passionate about their field. Even students with good grades and strong extracurricular involvement often feel anxious about whether they are doing the "right" things. The rapidly changing job market, especially with AI and global economic shifts, makes it even harder to plan a stable future or feel confident in long-term decisions.

To address this, universities should provide more flexible academic structures, interdisciplinary options, and stronger mentoring programs. Students need opportunities to explore different fields without fear of falling behind. Career counseling should begin in the first year, not just in the final semester. In addition, peer mentoring programs and mental health services can help students feel less isolated and more confident in their choices.

It's also important to change how we talk about success. College should not be seen only as a path to employment but as a place to develop identity, curiosity, and long-term goals. Uncertainty is not a weakness; it's a natural part of growth and exploration.

If we normalize this reality and provide the right support, students will feel more empowered to define success on their own terms, even if their path is not clear from the beginning. In the end, learning how to navigate uncertainty may be one of the most valuable lessons college can offer.

💡 My Reflections and Notes

Write down key insights, teaching ideas, personal reflections, or any information you want to remember.

Chapter 12

AI and the Future of Learning — Promise, Peril, and Possibility

Warm-Up

- Have you ever used ChatGPT or another AI tool to help you study or write something?
- What do you think are the advantages of learning with AI-powered tools or textbooks?
- Do you think students will still need teachers in the future when AI becomes more advanced?
- What concerns do you have about using AI in the classroom or for schoolwork?

Introduction

The classroom of the future is no longer a distant dream; it is already taking shape. Across Korea and the world, artificial intelligence (AI) is becoming a visible part of daily education. From AI tutors and chatbots to AI-powered learning platforms and digital textbooks, schools are beginning to explore new technologies to enhance learning. One of the biggest shifts is the introduction of AI Digital Textbooks (AIDT), interactive, adaptive materials that adjust to each student's pace and performance. These tools are designed to personalize learning, offer instant feedback, and support students in ways traditional textbooks never could.

However, this transformation has sparked deep controversy. Supporters of AIDT and AI tools argue that they can reduce educational inequality by giving every student access to a virtual tutor, improve motivation through customized learning paths, and help teachers focus more on emotional and social support. On the other hand, critics worry about overdependence on machines, loss of human interaction, digital distraction, and the erosion of critical thinking skills. Some educators fear that students may become passive learners, relying too much on AI to provide answers rather than thinking for themselves.

Academic honesty is another growing concern. With AI tools able to generate essays, solve math problems, and even complete entire assignments, issues like plagiarism and cheating have become more difficult to detect and define. Teachers are now faced with the challenge of rethinking how to evaluate learning in an AI-rich world, while students must consider the ethical limits of AI use. Questions of authorship, originality, and honesty are now more complex than ever before.

In addition, borderless online education enabled by AI and high-speed internet opens new opportunities but also raises questions about identity, discipline, and digital inequality. While some students thrive in online schools, others struggle with focus, motivation, and isolation. The balance between freedom and responsibility becomes harder to manage in virtual environments.

In this chapter, we will explore the potential and pitfalls of AI in education, focusing on how it affects learning, integrity, and the evolving roles of students and teachers in the digital age.

👤 Chitchat with Mates

1 Have you ever used AI to help with your homework? Did it help you learn better or just faster?

	Answers
Me	
Mate 1	
Mate 2	
Mate 3	

2 Do you think AI makes students more independent or more dependent? Why?

	Answers
Me	
Mate 1	
Mate 2	
Mate 3	

3 Should students be allowed to use AI tools like ChatGPT during class or exams?

	Answers
Me	
Mate 1	
Mate 2	
Mate 3	

4 If your future students use AI to write essays, how would you respond as their teacher?

	Answers
Me	
Mate 1	
Mate 2	
Mate 3	

 In-depth Reading

AI in Learning

Artificial Intelligence (AI) is no longer a distant future concept. It is here, transforming classrooms, textbooks, and the very definition of learning. In recent years, schools in Korea and around the world have introduced various forms of AI into their educational systems. Among the most significant innovations is the AI Digital Textbook (AIDT), an interactive, data-driven, and adaptive learning tool that responds to students' needs in real time. These tools promise to individualize learning, reduce teacher workload, and increase student motivation. However, they also raise important concerns about dependency, distraction, and educational integrity.

What Are AI Digital Textbooks?

Unlike traditional textbooks that present the same content to every student, AI Digital Textbooks are designed to be flexible and responsive. Using algorithms, they track each student's performance, identify areas of weakness, and suggest personalized learning activities. If a student struggles with grammar in English, the AIDT can automatically offer extra practice and explanations. If another student masters a math topic quickly, it can suggest more advanced problems. This personalized approach aims to close learning gaps and make education more efficient and engaging.

Korea has begun implementing AIDT in certain subjects like English, mathematics, and science. Proponents argue that this technology can help reduce the reliance on private tutoring by giving every student access to an individualized learning path, regardless of background. For teachers, AIDTs can function like a co-teacher, providing instant data on student progress and freeing up time for emotional support and creativity in the classroom.

Benefits of AI in the Classroom

The benefits of using AI in education are many. First, personalization allows students to learn at their own pace. Advanced learners can move ahead while struggling students receive targeted support. Second, AI tools offer immediate feedback, allowing students to correct mistakes in real time rather than waiting for the teacher to grade assignments. This can improve learning speed and retention.

Third, AI can make learning more interactive and enjoyable. Through gamified learning, simulations, and multimedia explanations, students can stay more engaged than with traditional lectures or paper textbooks. AI tools can also reduce teacher burnout by handling repetitive tasks like grading or data analysis, giving educators more time to focus on teaching strategy and student well-being.

Additionally, borderless online education is becoming more accessible thanks to AI and high-speed internet. Students can now take courses from foreign institutions, attend virtual classrooms, and learn from global instructors without leaving their homes. For students in rural or underserved areas, AI offers a gateway to opportunities that were once out of reach.

Risks and Controversies

Despite its advantages, the use of AI in education also comes with serious concerns. One of the biggest risks is overdependence. When students begin to rely too heavily on AI tools, they may lose the ability to think critically or solve problems independently. If an AI assistant always suggests the correct answer or rewrites their sentences, students may stop developing those skills themselves.

Another concern is digital distraction. While AI tools are meant to help learning, the use of digital devices can also make it easier for students to get distracted by games, videos, or social media, especially in online school environments. Without strong self-regulation, students may fall behind despite having access to advanced tools.

The issue of educational integrity is also growing. AI programs like ChatGPT can now generate full essays, solve math equations, and even produce computer code. While these tools are helpful for brainstorming or practice, they can also be misused. Students may submit AI-generated work as their own, raising questions about plagiarism and cheating. In such cases, traditional definitions of academic dishonesty may no longer be clear. Did the student write the essay, or did the AI? Should AI be considered a tool like a calculator, or a shortcut that undermines learning?

This uncertainty puts pressure on teachers. Many educators are unsure how to detect or respond to AI-assisted work. Should they ban it entirely, or accept it with certain conditions? Should they design assignments that AI cannot easily complete, such as oral presentations or in-class debates? These questions are still being debated across educational institutions.

Changing the Role of Teachers and Students

As AI becomes more present in education, the role of both teachers and students is being redefined. Teachers are no longer the sole source of knowledge but are becoming facilitators, guides, and mentors. Their job is not just to deliver content, but to help students make sense of information, think critically, and act ethically. They must also adapt to new classroom technologies, learn how to manage AI tools effectively, and maintain meaningful human relationships in increasingly digital learning spaces.

For students, learning is no longer about memorizing facts, but about knowing how to find, question, and use information responsibly. They must learn to work alongside AI rather than simply depend on it. This means developing digital literacy, including the ability to evaluate sources, detect bias in algorithms, and understand how AI systems work. Students must become more proactive, self-directed learners who can navigate vast digital resources with judgment and integrity.

Education systems must help students develop ethical awareness. Just because AI can do something doesn't mean it should be used that way. Schools need to teach students about honesty, authorship, and the long-term value of learning, not just about getting high scores with AI help. As AI becomes more powerful, human values must become even stronger to guide its use in meaningful and responsible ways.

Looking Ahead: Finding Balance

The future of education with AI will depend on balance. AI tools like AIDT have great potential to support learning, personalize instruction, and reduce inequality. But they must be used thoughtfully and ethically. Schools need clear policies on AI use, and teachers need proper training to integrate these tools wisely. Students, too, must learn how to use AI as a support, not a substitute for effort.

Moreover, equity must be considered. Not all students have access to reliable devices or internet connections, and overreliance on AI could widen the gap between privileged and underprivileged learners. Just as important as technological innovation is the human element: compassion, creativity, and community which no machine can fully replace. Ultimately, the most important lesson of AI in education may not be technological but moral. It challenges us to rethink what it means to learn, to create, and to be honest, not just with others, but with ourselves.

🔍 Comprehension Questions

1 What is an AI Digital Textbook, and how does it personalize learning for students?

_____

_____

2 What are two benefits AI can bring to students and teachers in a classroom setting?

_____

_____

3 Why is overdependence on AI a concern in education?

_____

_____

4 How does AI challenge traditional ideas of academic honesty and plagiarism?

_____

_____

5 What new roles are teachers expected to take on in AI-supported classrooms?

_____

_____

 **Ask AI**

How are AI tools treated in schools in the United Arab Emirates?

In-depth Discussion Questions

1 How can teachers balance the benefits of AI tools with the need to develop students' critical thinking, creativity, and independence in an AI-rich classroom?

2 In what ways might AI Digital Textbooks reduce educational inequality and in what ways might they unintentionally widen the gap between students of different backgrounds?

3 What practical strategies can schools and teachers use to prevent AI misuse, such as plagiarism or over-reliance on AI-generated content, while still encouraging responsible AI exploration?

4 How should assignments and assessments be redesigned to reflect real learning in a world where AI can generate essays, solve problems, and offer instant answers?

5 What skills should Korean students be taught to help them become ethical and literate users of AI technology in school and beyond?

6 How can teachers maintain meaningful student-teacher relationships and emotional support in classrooms that use AIDTs or online AI learning platforms extensively?

7 What role does digital literacy play in preparing students for future academic honesty? How can this be taught effectively across different grade levels?

8 If AI can personalize learning better than human instruction, what unique roles and responsibilities will teachers still need to fulfill in the classroom?

9 Make a discussion question based on the information you have obtained for "Ask AI."

🗨 Debate

1 Students should be allowed to use AI tools like ChatGPT in writing and homework assignments. (Focus: AI as a learning assistant vs. AI as a shortcut that replaces real effort)

Agree	Disagree

2 AI Digital Textbooks should replace traditional textbooks in all Korean middle and high schools. (Focus: personalized, interactive learning vs. loss of traditional structure and equality)

Agree	Disagree

3 AI use in schools encourages cheating and should be restricted through strict school policies. (Focus: promoting honesty through regulation vs. teaching students to use AI ethically)

Agree	Disagree

4 Online AI-powered schools will eventually replace physical classrooms. (Focus: flexible, borderless learning vs. loss of social interaction and school community)

Agree	Disagree

Wrap-Up: Your Turn to Write

Prompt: *What do you think is the most important benefit or risk of using AI in education? As a future teacher, how would you respond to that benefit or risk in your own classroom?*

Sample Essay

I think the most important benefit of using AI in education is personalized learning. Every student learns differently, and AI tools like digital textbooks can adjust to a student's level, speed, and learning style. As someone who struggled with math in high school, I can imagine how helpful it would have been to get instant feedback and extra practice designed just for me. AI could help students become more confident and motivated because they don't have to feel left behind or bored in class. It can also help students learn independently, without always relying on the teacher or private tutoring. This kind of individualized support can make education more inclusive, especially for students who need extra time or a different approach.

However, this benefit also brings a new responsibility for teachers. Personalized learning through AI does not mean that teachers become less important. In fact, I believe our role becomes even more meaningful. Teachers need to guide students in how to use AI tools effectively, make sure they are not just clicking through answers, and encourage deeper thinking. We also need to help students stay honest. Some may be tempted to copy AI-generated answers without understanding the content. That's why teachers should focus more on project-based learning, class discussions, and oral presentations—activities where AI cannot do all the work. These methods can also help teachers truly understand what each student has learned, both in terms of knowledge and personal growth.

In my future classroom, I want to use AI as a support tool, not a replacement. I will encourage students to use AI for practice, research, and brainstorming, but I will also teach them how to think critically and solve problems independently. I will create a learning environment where AI supports creativity rather than limits it. I believe that AI can be a powerful partner in education, but only if students learn how to use it with responsibility, curiosity, and honesty. In the end, AI should help students become better learners and more thoughtful individuals, not just faster test takers.

💡 My Reflections and Notes

Write down key insights, teaching ideas, personal reflections, or any information you want to remember.

Epilogue

Beyond the Debate: Becoming the Teachers Our Students Need

Throughout this book, we have examined the multifaceted, often contentious landscape of English education in Korea. From early childhood immersion programs to AI-powered digital classrooms, from the pressures of the CSAT to the promise of the International Baccalaureate, each chapter has invited you not just to analyze issues, but to reflect on what kind of educator you aspire to become.

What emerges from these discussions is not a single solution or philosophy, but a deep truth: education is a human endeavor, shaped by relationships, values, and evolving societal needs. As Korea grapples with demographic shifts, technological transformations, and global uncertainty, the role of the teacher remains essential, but it is also changing. Today's educators must be flexible facilitators, culturally aware guides, and ethical innovators. They must be ready to empower students, not merely instruct them.

The future of English education in Korea does not rest solely on curriculum changes or government policy. It will be shaped by the daily decisions and convictions of teachers, teachers like you, who choose empathy over efficiency, equity over tradition, and inquiry over indifference. You will be the ones who interpret policy into practice, who balance parental concerns with professional insight, and who help students see English not as a test to pass, but as a tool to connect with the world and with themselves.

This second edition reflects my own ongoing learning journey, one enriched by classroom experience, conversations with students and colleagues, and yes, the thoughtful use of AI in shaping this book's clarity and accessibility. In that spirit, I invite you to carry forward the debates, not as arguments to win, but as dialogues to deepen. Question assumptions. Share your voice. Support your students. And most of all, never forget that meaningful change often begins not in policies or programs, but in the quiet, consistent courage of teachers who care.

Thank you for walking this path with me.

Park Jai Young, Ph.D.

Debates on English Education 2nd edition
영어교육토론 개정판

초 판 1쇄 발행 2021년 9월 30일
개정판 1쇄 발행 2025년 8월 20일

지 은 이 | 박재영
펴 낸 이 | 김진수
펴 낸 곳 | 한국문화사
등   록 | 제1994-9호
주   소 | 서울시 성동구 아차산로49, 404호 (성수동1가, 서울숲코오롱디지털타워3차)
전   화 | 02-464-7708
팩   스 | 02-499-0846
이 메 일 | hkm7708@daum.net
홈페이지 | http://hph.co.kr

ISBN 979-11-6919-336-8 93740

· 이 책의 내용은 저작권법에 따라 보호받고 있습니다.
· 잘못된 책은 구매처에서 바꾸어 드립니다.
· 책값은 뒤표지에 있습니다.

오류를 발견하셨다면 이메일이나 홈페이지를 통해 제보해주세요.
소중한 의견을 모아 더 좋은 책을 만들겠습니다.